THE FIGHTING DOC

The Rhodesian Bush War Diary of John Coey
KIA 19 July 1975

John Alan Coey

30° South Publishers (Pty) Ltd

Helion & Company Ltd

Published in 2015 by:

30° SOUTH PUBLISHERS (PTY) LTD.
16 Ivy Road
Pinetown 3610
South Africa
email: info@30degreessouth.co.za
website: www.30degreessouth.co.za

and

HELION & COMPANY LTD.
26 Willow Road
Solihull
West Midlands
B91 1UE
England
Tel. 0121 705 3393 Fax 0121 711 4075
email: info@helion.co.uk
website: www.helion.co.uk

Designed & typeset by SA Publishing Services / kerrincocks@gmail.com
Cover design by Kerrin Cocks
Map by Phil Wright
Printed in the UK by Lightning Source
Printed in South Africa by Pinetown Printers

ISBN RSA: 978-1-928211-65-5
ISBN UK: 978-1-910294-96-3
ebook:978-1-928211-66-2

British Library Cataloguing-in-Publication Data
A catalogue record for this book is available from the British Library

Cover image: An iconic photo of John with the American flag on a summit in Rhodesia, perhaps how he would like to be remembered.

The other night I dreamed I returned home
after getting out of the army.
Cpl. John Alan Coey November 12, 1950 - July 19, 1975

Where the battle rages, there the loyalty of the soldier is proved;
and to be steady on all the battlefield besides,
is merely flight and disgrace if he flinches at that point.
—Martin Luther

To the 100,000 American dead of Korea and Vietnam
who were betrayed by their own government.
To those who have sought meaning and purpose in life,
and truth in an age of deceit, deception and conspiracy.
Remember the fundamental truth of Jesus Christ, I am the Way,
The truth, and the Life. No man cometh unto the Father except by me.
—Corporal John Alan Coey
Rhodesian Light Infantry
Born: 12 November 1950
Killed in action: 19 July 1975

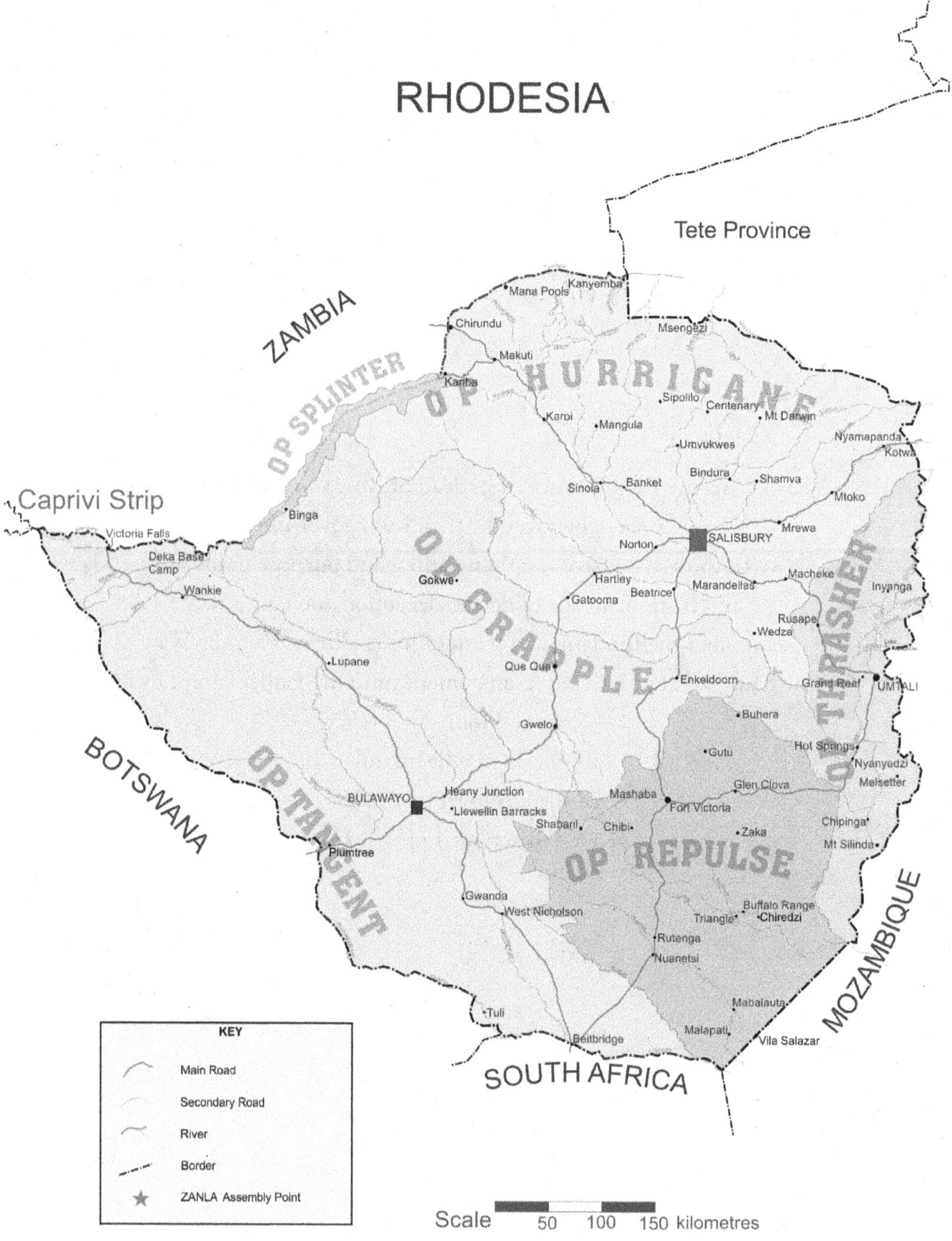
RHODESIA
Tete Province
ZAMBIA
Caprivi Strip
BOTSWANA
SOUTH AFRICA
MOZAMBIQUE
OP SPLINTER
OP HURRICANE
OP GRAPPLE
OP THRASHER
OP TANGENT
OP REPULSE
Kanyemba
Mana Pools
Chirundu
Makuti
Kariba
Msengezi
Sipolilo
Centenary
Mt Darwin
Karoi
Mangula
Umvukwes
Nyamapanda
Kotwa
Bindura
Shamva
Sinoia
Banket
Mtoko
Binga
Victoria Falls
Deka Base Camp
Wankie
Norton
SALISBURY
Mrewa
Hartley
Gatooma
Beatrice
Marandellas
Macheke
Inyanga
Gokwe
Rusape
Wedza
Lupane
Que Que
Enkeldoorn
Grand Reef
UMTALI
Buhera
Gwelo
Gutu
Hot Springs
Nyanyadzi
Melsetter
Glen Clova
Mashaba
Fort Victoria
BULAWAYO
Heany Junction
Llewellin Barracks
Shabani
Chibi
Zaka
Chipinga
Mt Silinda
Plumtree
Gwanda
West Nicholson
Buffalo Range
Triangle
Chiredzi
Rutenga
Nuanetsi
Mabalauta
Tuli
Malapati
Beitbridge
Vila Salazar
KEY
Main Road
Secondary Road
River
Border
ZANLA Assembly Point
Scale 50 100 150 kilometres

CONTENTS

FOREWORD

The late John Alan Coey, author of this journal, was perhaps one of the most gifted writers and thinkers of the 20th century. He wrote virtually all of this material between his 21st and 24th years. He was an American who believed Christian freedom was worth fighting for and, in his case, worth dying for. John understood that the financial oligarchy is selling out the free world to buy a world government. You could not, in good conscience, support the internationalist Vietnam War where cynical financiers were sending American boys to be cannon fodder to further the Red Revolution, rather than truly end it. Therefore, John made what his brother Ed called 'perhaps the most unusual protest to the Vietnam War'. John was not a coward. He did not flee to Canada or even into a materialistic, hedonistic lifestyle, like many of his contemporaries. Rather, he chose to support Rhodesia in its struggle against communism. He flew there the day after he graduated from Ohio State University in 1972. Those who would call him a 'mercenary' need to know that he was paid 100 dollars a month for most of his time there. John was a marked man from the start. The same hidden hand behind Vietnam was also guaranteeing Rhodesia's fall. That force mysteriously washed out John from officers' training as well as the elite SAS. Why? Because John towered above his peers in understanding the real causes of the Red Revolution and communicated them well in talks and articles. He also loved a pure life, dedicated to the Lord Jesus Christ. The enemy found nothing with which to blackmail him. He eventually found his niche as a Fireforce medic in the RLI, who went into combat with his men to tend to them as soon as they were wounded. He was killed on 19 July 1975, while attempting to save such a life. 'Greater love hath no man than this, that a man lay down his life for his friends'. (John 15:13)

This book was compiled from an article of John's (Chapter 1); his 'Soldiers Protest'(Chapter 2); a daily journal he kept on the field, plus his letters home (Chapters 3–31); an eyewitness account of his death, and his brother's message at his Rhodesian military funeral (Chapter 32); and selected portions from several striking letters of tribute afterward, from the hundreds the Coey family received (Chapter 33). The poem on the back cover was written in memory of some of his buddies killed in battle before he was. His family found it written in the back of a World War II prayer book given him by his mother when he left for Rhodesia. Photos in the book are either those John took, or buddies took of him with his camera. The cover photo is of John planting his American flag on Inyangani, the highest mountain in Rhodesia (see Chapter 6). The honest reader who loves God and freedom is in for a real treat. John's journal is great literature: spiritually uplifting, morally and politically discerning, emotionally cleansing and moving. John's extraordinary dedication to the Lord Jesus Christ and Christian freedom make him a superb role model for a generation that has few. 'Now he belongs to the ages', as it was said of Abraham Lincoln the night he was assassinated. 'Verily, verily, I say unto you, except a corn of wheat fall into the ground and die, it abideth alone; but if it die, it bringeth forth much fruit'. (John 12:24)

Pat Brookes
NPL Editor

PREFACE

"Supreme excellence in warfare consists in
breaking the enemy's will to resist."
—Sun Tzu

What has become known as the Vietnam era was a period marked by rabid protest. Each day on the television, hysterical and unwashed anti-war demonstrators paraded before the American people as the news commentators pontificated about the protesters' moral commitment to stop the killing in Vietnam. Of course, now that Indochina has been captured, and the communal butchery of entire populations has begun, not even the faintest side of dismay can be heard from either the noble mobs or the gentlemen of the media. Unfortunately, neither the deluded apostles of peace who roamed the street at that time, nor the perplexed silent majority who watched their antics, had the slightest notion of what was really happening before their eyes. If either group ever wondered why a government engaged in active warfare against communist forces in Vietnam, or was at the same time busy pumping massive economic transfusions to shaky communist regimes all over the planet, and indirectly to North Vietnam itself, they quickly put the thought out of mind. For none of them realized that the war in Vietnam was actually a war on America. The broad mass of Americans never became informed enough to know that they were victims of psychological warfare. They were never aware that they had been forced into playing an old political game called the 'choice between false alternatives'. The country had been artificially divided between the hawks and the doves; between those who supported the government's war and those who opposed it; between military-industrial conservatives and campus ivory-tower liberals. These were the sides, and each citizen was supposed to choose between a protracted no-win slaughter, and a humiliating surrender. Either choice led to the same result, demoralization of the American people. Therein lay the true purpose of the war. No-one was supposed to know that America has been programmed to lose, and her people conditioned into psychological demoralization. The gradual wasting away of the will to resist, that is why it was decided that one of the smallest and most underdeveloped of all the communist satraps would defeat the United States. The confused and puzzled American people would never know the control of the national government had already slipped from their hands in a secret and bloodless seizure of power in 1913. They would never learn that the government policies are made by the mysterious agents of even more mysterious family dynasties, such as the Rockefellers and the Rothschilds, who long ago carved up the world into economic spheres of influence. They would never fathom the horrible truth that wars such as Vietnam are planned for profit, power, and demoralization. But why demoralization? Because the ultimate goal of the family dynasties is to create a world-governing monopoly-cartel system of economic power in which labour will be cheap, because labour will be slave. To become a part of this system, America must be reduced in status and power so that she can be comfortably merged with the Soviet Union. But the American people will never be comfortably merged until they have been brainwashed into believing that resistance is futile. But during the Vietnam era there was one young American who understood demoralization by the choice of false alternatives. His name was John Alan Coey, and he was determined to resist being manipulated by the hostile and alien forces which had captured his government. John Alan Coey grew up in the American age of optimism. The America of the 1950s was a period of relative tranquillity, of a return to normalcy following the upheavals of World War II and the Korean conflict.

The boys had come home, most of them, and they were settling down, establishing families, and pursuing the American dream. Technologically, America was progressing at an unprecedented rate, and public opinion was self-assured that our future held only better things to come. All one needs to do was to take advantage of educational opportunities, work hard, and the good life would be his. Few people were pessimistic. Such was the national outlook during John Alan Coey's youth. Reared in a stable family, he grew up in middle-class, suburban USA, and he shared the optimistic outlook of Middle America. He was a faithful member of his church, an above-average student at his neighbourhood school, and active in the Boy Scouts. By the time he was in high school, he had taken up athletics, running in both track and cross-country, and he had joined the marching band, playing the trumpet and the sousaphone. In the Boy Scouts he achieved all of the highest awards: Eagle Scout, Pro Deo et Patria, Order of the Arrow (Honorary Fraternity), and Hornaday Award, the rare medal given for achievement in conservation. He also served for several summers, with distinction, on the staff of the Boy Scout reservation. He was obviously a young man on the way. However, by the time John finished high school, American involvement in the Vietnam war was well into its fourth year, and what had once been an obscure area of the world to most Americans, was now being branded into the national conscience. The Tet offensive would remind us that we had been embroiled in far more than just a police action. The Student Protest Movement, spawned by the communist underground and initiated at Berkeley in 1964, had spread to all the major college campuses. America, under the influence of student demonstrations in the universities and 'civil-rights' riots in the big cities, was losing her innocent optimism of the 1950s to these calculated insurrections.

It was in this milieu that John entered the Ohio State University in the autumn of 1968. His love for conservation had become so deep-rooted that he majored in forestry. But he was now grown, and time for the carefree activities of youth was over. He was an eye-witness to major anti-war and black-power riots on campus, and, as if those did not disgust him enough, he had become aware that the Vietnam war was designed to guarantee communist victory in Indochina.

During his four years of the university, the war dragged on according to ignominious plan, and the American people, drenched in propaganda and accustomed to winning quickly, tired and sickened of the entire farcical show, until even the most strident hawks could barely be heard to utter a word in its defence. Meanwhile, John had begun serious consideration of a military career, and had entered the Marine NROTC programme at Ohio State University. In the summer of 1971, he participated in the Marine training camp at Quantico, Virginia. The climate at that time was such that the young officer recruits were warned not to wear their uniforms in their own nation's capital of Washington DC, for fear of being shot by urban terrorists.

As John approached graduation day, he was faced with a momentous decision. To either remain in the armed forces of the US, or to find an alternative. US service would certainly mean he is being used as a pawn by the secret oligarchy in its Vietnam travesty. Joining the ranks of the draft dodgers fleeing in droves to Canada and Europe, would mean he was being used as a puppet in the communist drive to destroy US military organization and preparedness. Not wishing to be caught in either of these traps, John decided to take the most honourable course available to him; one that would effectively protest the Vietnam demoralization program being implemented in tandem by the government and those ostensibly against the government. He embarked on a course neither disloyal to his people nor cowardly to his own soul. He surveyed the whole world in order to find one country that he thought to be honestly fighting communism and defending the heritage of the West. His choice was Rhodesia, and there he hoped he would not find treachery. John graduated from the Ohio State University in March of 1972, and immediately left for Rhodesia. He had already made arrangements to join the Rhodesian army, and upon his departure from America he sent his draft board, the Marines, government officials, and the press, an eloquent statement entitled *'A Soldiers Protest'*, which the reader will find herein. John's story, told in his own words, begins with that protest and continues to his last valiant struggle on 19 July 1975. As the reader proceeds, he or she will soon notice that the young American soldier was little understood by most Rhodesians. Sad to say, John was not appreciated until he had made the ultimate sacrifice.

The chronicles herein describe the incredible hardships, and sometimes the scorn and ridicule, which he endured and endured. He had hoped to find a country in which the people are fully alert to the grave mortal danger to the West posed by those Siamese twins, communism and internationalism. Instead, he found a people almost as pathetic and soporific as his own Americans. True, he found a few Rhodesians awake, but generally he found a people too narrowly provincial to fully appreciate the worldwide implications of the savage attack being unleashed against their small country. The reader will not fail to grasp the significance of the fall of Portuguese Africa (Mozambique and Angola), which impending disaster John follows carefully in his journals, through to the final gasp of agony. But not even this monumental blow to Rhodesian security seemed to arouse a lethargic people; little more than the fall of Cuba seemed to arouse the American people. Considering the mounting danger and the stakes involved, John's discovery of an unconcerned nation that should have been mobilizing to the hilt, accounts for his vacillation about what he should do personally. The question which constantly plagued him was the extent of his obligation to a people who were sometimes antagonistic toward his efforts to help or warn them. Nonetheless, there was deep within his soul an urge to persevere, to seek his destiny in an Africa he had come to love. As a participant in over sixty Fireforce missions, he finally found it. John's one ambition was to become an officer, and, as the reader will note, he was progressing through the year-long course towards his goal, when he was suddenly struck down by some hidden hand. John never lost sight of his mission to warn the Rhodesian people about the international conspiracy, and he did so openly in an article, *The Myth of American Anti-communism*, which was published in the Rhodesian army journal *Assegai*. Not long after the publication of this monograph, it was labelled subversive, because Rhodesian policymakers are afraid to deny the fact that the American citadel has been captured. John's reward was dismissal from the officers' course. This was a crushing blow to his morale, and most men would have left the country in disgust. Indeed, this writer urged him to come home at once. But John persisted and returned to the SAS where he seems to have received an unkindly welcome.

Unwanted there, he finally applied for the medics' course, and again the hidden hand struck. Someone approached the course instructor and urged him not to accept John's application, but the instructor would hear none of it, and so John found a home in the army at last. After completing the medics' course, he returned to active duty, but found life in the basecamps a bore. Thus, he initiated a new role in the commandos, that of Fireforce medic. John wanted to be with his men where and when they were wounded, and he saved many lives. But he also wanted to be on the scene so that if he could not save a man's life, he might witness to that man about Jesus Christ, and save his eternal soul. For this commitment John ultimately sacrificed his own life, as he died with a wounded comrade in his arms.

The reader will discern that a ceasefire had been called by the politicians late in 1974, just as the security forces were on the verge of complete victory. A period of so-called détente settled in, but lasted only long enough for the communists to retrench. Thus, a very peculiar pattern emerged, one which was most familiar to observers of the Vietnam War, snatching a reprieve for sagging communist forces out of the jaws of victory. So John became another victim of détente, and the lines he so often quoted came to apply to himself: 'We never lost. We were always betrayed'.

One day John had hoped to publish a book about his Rhodesian adventure and he kept a daily journal of his experiences and impressions for that purpose. Unfortunately, at the time of his death he had entrusted both his journals and photograph album to an American girl whom he regarded as a good friend. Upon learning that John had been killed, she became frightened because she might be in possession of sensitive material, and turned over everything to her superior in The Evangelical Alliance Mission, TEAM. They gave the properties to the chairman of TEAM, a Canadian, who was working closely with the Rhodesian Special Branch. All three missionaries formed their own opinion that the journals and photos should be forwarded to the Special Branch for 'review'. These actions were taken without ever consulting or notifying John's family, who were en route to Rhodesia for the express purpose of obtaining his journals, as well as for his funeral. In fact, the full story of the disappearance of this personal property was not revealed until 31 May 1977.

The Special Branch did a thorough review, and the mutilated remains of the journals were finally returned by persons unknown to John's family, nearly a full year after his death. It cannot be ascertained how much was censored, but in some places three to four months were missing, and the generous reviewers left not a single word from 1975. The uncensored portions will be found herein, but the family has supplemented lost sections with John's carefully preserved letters. Now his dream of one day publishing his book has come true, despite all obstacles. Late in 1974, Professor Revilo P. Oliver of the University of Illinois wrote a most prescient letter to John, in which he said, "Yours is the choice of Achilles." Those who have read the Homeric epic will recall that the gods gave the Achaean hero, Achilles, a choice to lead a long life with little accomplishment, or to perish in battle at a young age, but with everlasting glory. Such was the choice of an American hero who unquestionably believed that the quality of a man's life is far more important than its quantity. Why did John Alan Coey go to Rhodesia?

To make the most unique and significant protest against the Vietnam War, it is true. But more to the point, he went to fight for his people. He firmly believed that the men of the Christian West are one, that there is a unity among them which transcends nationalism, and that the answer to usurpers and tyrants has always been, 'Defiance, traitors, who hurl in your teeth'. Our kinsmen in Rhodesia are in mortal danger, and so, John Alan Coey journeyed to the very frontier of Christendom to say to the New Barbarians, 'You shall not pass'. He never received a medal, or an equivalent to the Purple Heart, but he was unafraid to sacrifice his life, because in his heart and soul was written the code of chivalry of the soldier of the West.

G. Edward Coey
Hide Away Hills, Ohio

CHAPTER ONE
Christian Activism

July 1977

May 1970 witnessed the mobilizing of the New Left in universities all over America to protest the US invasion of Cambodia. On the campus of Ohio State University, Black Power, Gay Lib, Students for a Democratic Society, the Weathermen, the Student Non-violent Coordinating Committee, and various other leftist ad-hoc groups were calling for a student strike to shut the school down. The administration building was stoned. National Guard and Highway Patrol units were called in to stop the rioting. The phalanx of police was pelted with eggs, bricks and tack balls, and retaliated with tear gas, rubber pellets and buckshot. Rioting spread to the neighbouring community. Shops were looted and burned, windows smashed, telephone booths overturned, fire hydrants broken, and roads blocked. The academic world was in a rage, because on the campus to the north panicky guardsmen shot down four students at Kent State. What was a Christian student to do? Like many students of the so-called 'megaversities', I felt the urgency to find a reason to live, the need for activism and commitment, the necessity to right injustice, to protest against pollution, the futility of the Vietnam War, and to show that the human race was in trouble. I wanted the American dream of freedom and success to be realized also. I saw, however, that the moratoriums, demonstrations, student strikes, peace marches, Earth Days, and May Day revolutions were organised by professional revolutionaries, and financed by the leftist foundations of Ford, Carnegie, and Rockefeller to foment the semblance of street revolution. The assessment of the dehumanizing trends of industrial society was correct, but the answer was not in the culture that offered escape in drugs, psychedelics, hard rock, hippy communes, freak-outs, and Eastern religions that rejected the reality of the physical universe. If changes were to be made, Christian activism was needed to change hearts through the Gospel of Christ. Many Christians interpret these times as being the prelude to the second coming of Christ. There is a convincing argument that such events as the Zionist takeover of Palestine, the World Wars, the increase in knowledge and travel, the rise of

Russia and communist conquests, the rise of the Ecumenical Church, occultism, and apostasy, are the fulfilment of biblical prophecy for the end times. It all seems to fit. Yet there is a strong argument that these things have happened before, such as during the collapse of the Roman Empire, and during the Middle Ages, and that we are now witnessing the decline of Western civilization.

At issue is a contest of faiths. We see the world in crisis because the impact of science and technology has displaced belief in the supernatural; a faith in God. An alternative faith has arisen, the faith in man as the creative intelligence of the world, who by the force of his rational intelligence can redirect his destiny and reorganize his life and world. By denying God, man becomes the most 'intelligent' of beings. This is the vision and faith shared by communists, socialists, fellow-travellers, liberals and humanists, the belief in the self-sufficiency of man with his power of reason and science to guide his progress. The main difference is that communists are willing to suffer the penalties of their crimes. They see the world crisis as the frustration of the world unable to stand still, but unwilling to go forward to the logical end of technological civilization – communism. It is said the crisis of the Western world is the degree that it has separated itself from God, and shares the faith of the communists. The crisis of the communist world is the degree it has failed to separate its people from God. The stronger faith will win.

What must a Christian do?

Prayer meetings, bible studies, church services, singing choruses and witnessing, are all vital to develop faith. But Christians must grasp current issues and not withdraw from world affairs, nor fail to resist or even protest what they know to be wrong, for fear of getting political. Although a period of tribulation is foreseen, many do nothing to stop it, and expect to be spared by a 'rapture' of saints. The opposition to the leftward swing of governments, seminaries, and universities is insufficient and ineffective, or else the faith in men would not have become the dominating belief of the leftists who have become clergy, professors and politicians. Very few world leaders publicly proclaim Christian faith. Many theologians deny the divinity of Christ, and even proclaim God is dead. Christianity is ridiculed at the universities, where the best minds are turned off God. Prayer alone, without action, may be insufficient, for God works through his created beings. The Hungarians did not actively resist the Soviet takeover, and were shot in the head while praying for deliverance.

Just as the prophets condemned the wickedness of Israel and Judah, John the Baptist publicly condemned Herod. As Christ condemned the scribes and Pharisees, so must the churches and individual Christians condemn the evils of today. The Dutch Bible smuggler, Brother Andrew, says persecution of all religions in communist countries is worse than ever, because Western leaders do not condemn it for fear of jeopardizing détente. Western Christians forget about their persecuted brothers. Christians can be effective in public life, just as Joseph, Moses, Joshua, David, Solomon, Daniel and Mordecai were great warriors, lawgivers, kings, governors, judges, and even empire builders, besides being prophets. Christians must become these too, and not abandon public professions to the non-believers. Communism can be stopped. It can be stopped on the ground by our soldiers. It can be stopped in the world capitals and universities if more Christians become professors and participate in government. The West does not have to merge with the Communist Bloc to make a new world order. That will not bring peace, but make the terrors of communism universal. Is not freedom of religion preferable to worshipping in an underground church with threat of persecution, informers, and secret police? Since 1917 the Soviets alone have murdered an estimated thirty-five million people, and the souls of millions more because the youth are indoctrinated with atheism. The Red Chinese have murdered thirty million more. Communism threatens to uproot Christianity wherever found, and is the greatest threat to the Gospel in the history of Christendom. Western civilization is based on Christianity. The decline of the West correlates to its demise, and the West can be revived by a revival of faith. Is it worth saving in southern Africa? Although it has many faults, Western civilization has exhibited by its history the ability to produce culture in its great art, music, poetry, literature, sculpture and architecture; all expressions of soul in contact with God. Systems of law and government have been devised, permitting a reasonable amount of liberty. Existence has been made more than a struggle for survival. The black African has his culture also, but white rule has not repressed it. He is free to choose his lifestyle, whether in the bush or metropolis, and judging from the multitudes that swarm to the cities, many prefer at least some aspect of Western life. Does communism offer a better alternative? This century started off being the most promising of all history, yet in less than thirty years the world has been brought to the brink of a new dark age of terror and barbarism. God will be merciful if we repent. A Christian triumph in the West, communist world, and the Middle East, could change everything. If, as Brother Andrew says, we do not take the Gospel to the communists and the heathen, they will come to us as revolutionists. They are already here. Are you willing to back up your faith by action? Is your faith in God and civilization stronger than the communist faith? Is it worth living and fighting for? I think it is.

CHAPTER 2
A Soldier's Protest

This writer [John] requested and received a discharge from the US Marine Corps Platoon Leaders' Class, Officer Training Program, and upon graduation from the Ohio State University, enlisted in Rhodesian commandos to protest the following:

1. The deliberate prevention by the US government of victory over communist forces in Southeast Asia.
2. The attempted overthrow of the constitutional republic of the United States by a revolutionary conspiracy of internationalists, collectivists and communists, in and out of the US government.
3. The attempted destruction by government defence officials of the fighting capabilities of American combat forces.
4. The United States could have won the two wars communist forces since World War II, except for the deliberate prevention of victory by the civilian authorities who have usurped the power to make technical military decisions. During the Korean War, the Truman administration denied General MacArthur victory over Korean and Chinese communists, and relieved him of commands. Similarly, the Johnson and Nixon administrations have prevented victory over the Viet Cong and North Vietnamese forces by restricting offences on the harbours, supply centres, and manufacturing sites.

   In spite of the Soviet military build-up, the Defence Department has reduced the fighting capabilities of American armed forces, not only by disarmament programmes, but by cancelling development of a nuclear-powered fleet, and bomber, missile, and spacecraft attack systems. Officials in the departments of the army, navy, and air force have damaged discipline, morale, militarism, and training standards by fostering 'civilization' programmes that have perpetrated race riots, narcotic addiction, 'fragging' and killing of officers. This involves the throwing of fragmentation hand grenades by their own enlisted men. Sometimes combat units refused to fight.

   This consistent undermining of the military is not misjudgement or mistake, but deliberate sabotage. It is part of the attempt to bring the United States underworld government by subverting the sovereignty and independence of the constitutional Republic of the United States. Elimination of the military services as effective defence and as anti-communist elements in the nation, is necessary to neutralize resistance to the revolutionary forces of the Council on Foreign Relations and the international financial establishment that control the policies and programmes of civilian authorities and high-ranking military personnel.

I prefer not to serve in the United States armed forces since that service would not benefit my country, but only its enemies. Protest and resistance of current military policies from within the ranks is ineffective because of no public backing and repression by civilian authorities; eg Generals MacArthur, LeMay and Walker, and Admiral Anderson, were relieved of their commands when they protested against the policies of the Defence Department. Civil control may be necessary to guard against military dictatorships and juntas, but civilian authorities and politicians deserve obedience and loyalty only when they, too, are loyal to the Republic and respect the nation's freedom. Although the military may be rendered unfit for war, it may still be used to enforce totalitarian government if made a part of the UN peacekeeping forces. No solder is obliged to serve revolutionaries, opportunists, and subversives attempting to break all constitutional restraints on the power of government.

Since I do not object to military service, I choose to serve in the Rhodesian army where I may perhaps help sustain European civilization in Africa. Although this action has cost me an officer's commission, and though my citizenship may be revoked, this is the most I can do for my country under the circumstances.

America and all the Western nations are in a civilization crisis manifested by the confrontation between Christianity and communism, liberty and totalitarian government, national sovereignty and internationalism, conservatism and liberalism. The civilization crisis is a life-and-death struggle for world power of the alien forces of international finance, and the existence of the west; now weakened not only by liberal pacifism and moral decadence, but by treason in governmental, educational, and religious institutions. Every officer and enlisted man has sworn allegiance to both the constitution and the president. That oath of allegiance is exclusive now, and each must choose either to fight for the liberty of the republic or serve the correct oligarchy that intends to destroy it. I wish only to help Americans regain control of the destiny of our country.

CHAPTER 3
Flight to Rhodesia and Basic Training

John writes his first letter from Rhodesia to his family in America:

26 March 1972

I am now posted at the commando school just outside Salisbury, where I will begin a nineteen-week course of basic training. The barracks here are very modern, almost like an apartment complex. The army is cosmopolitan. Soldiers are her from Germany, England, Portugal, Zambia, and South Africa, but the bulk is Rhodesian. There are also a few Americans, only one of whom I have met. He is from Cleveland, Ohio, but of Zambian origin, and has an African name I don't remember. He was in the United States Marines and served in Vietnam. After deserting from a Marine camp, he fled here and enlisted, but not for any good motives. I must have been asked a hundred times why I came here, but no-one is really surprised. All are friendly and very curious about the US Marines. One group, just finished training, completed a ten-mile run with full pack, helmet, boots, and rifle.

I had a very enjoyable and interesting flight that seemed like a pilgrimage. As I left Columbus with a mighty sweep over the city, I could see sites which flashed to mind memories of past times there. I could see the hills to the south, and as the plane looped from west to east, I first spotted the downtown area, the university, and even my high school, Brookhaven, and Northland shopping centre, all in a few moments before passing into the clouds and the intensely blue stratosphere.

Later, when the clouds cleared, I could see the mining country of Pennsylvania and the farmlands of New York. My plane flew into Boston at sunset; directly over Boston harbour, dotted with islands, some having lighthouses. Just before touchdown, I could see a silhouette of the city against the red sunset.

After staying in Boston for three hours, that night I flew on a 747 Jumbo for England. The skies had cleared, and over Boston a bright crescent moon shone, with Venus directly below it. The lights of the city sparkled and twinkled like bulbs on a Christmas tree. Lights outlined the coastal islands surrounded by the great black abyss of the ocean.

I woke up again at seven in the morning, BMT, or one o'clock your time, still flying over the ocean. I could see a spectacular array of stars, but could only recognise the constellation Cassiopeia. Way off to the east appeared the thin blue arc of dawn, which gradually grew until it slowly engulfed the entire sky. The horizon turned pink until the sun emerged, shining on the rippling of the ocean. As the plane approached Ireland, oil slicks appeared in dark blotches on the ocean surface. Clouds hid Ireland, but the sky cleared over the Irish Sea. I had a tremendous view of the English countryside; brown and green polygon-shaped patches divided by hedgerows, which gave the entire scene a jigsaw-puzzle appearance. Heathrow airport is twenty miles from the city, but our landing was delayed, so we circled London for several minutes. The city is immense and widely dispersed, but it doesn't seem densely crowded.

It was a warm sunny day, and I spent most of the next twelve hours visiting London on foot. Most of the time I spent in one place, Westminster Abbey. The exterior is impressive, with its flying buttresses and grandiose architecture, but the interior is a most awe-inspiring sight. It creates the deepest reverence and admiration for our early Western civilization. There are towering columns, vaults and domes, and stained-glass windows depicting Christ and the saints. Gothic architecture is, I believe, a superb symbol of the West.

Inside are buried the great warriors, statesmen, poets, musicians, and scientists of Britain. Names like Burns, Newton, Gladstone, Blake, Handel, the Brontes, and Wordsworth. Too many to remember. The tombs and monuments blend perfectly into the architecture. Some lie underneath giant stones in the floor which carry inscriptions. Others are buried in the walls, and some even in a base of altars. Several are so old that the inscriptions have worn away entirely. The tomb of England's Unknown Soldier is there also.

I hope the heritage and tradition, so evident and abundant here, will inspire new greatness in England. I'm glad I came first, to see the source of the civilization for which I will be fighting in southern Africa.

I left London at night, and thus missed seeing Europe, the Mediterranean, North Africa, the Sahara, and the Sudan.

The flight to Johannesburg offered the best view of Africa. One could see Mount Kilimanjaro towering above the clouds, the peak capped in white. We were now in the Southern Hemisphere. The Serengeti plains of Tanzania stretched to the horizon, vast, lush and green, but sparsely vegetated in some places. Later we flew parallel to what appeared to be an inland sea. This was Lake Malawi. Even at our altitude, we could not see the eastern shoreline, only blue water from the west to the eastern horizon.

As we flew over Rhodesia and South Africa, I noticed that the land is more green and lush. The plane landed in Johannesburg at two o'clock on Monday afternoon. After I learned that it takes two days for the train ride to Salisbury, I bought another plane ticket for the north. The flight from Nairobi to Johannesburg had passed directly over Salisbury, but the 747 had not stopped there.

On the way to South Africa, I spoke with a young Rhodesian aged about nineteen. He is very liberal, and spoke of the new order, and of changing the ills of society. He apparently does not believe in God or the fallibility of man. I do not believe that he is typical, but this does demonstrate that the same liberal and collectivist teachings of American universities are also espoused in Rhodesia, with success.

I left Johannesburg at half past four, and arrived in Salisbury at six o'clock in the middle of a thunderstorm. After checking in with the immigration officer, I was met by the army and put up for the night at an army barracks in Salisbury. The next morning I went to [King] George VI Barracks, where I was sworn in, and completed forms and papers for registration. Major Lamprecht swore me in, but I did not have a chance to talk with him. I proceeded immediately to the chief military base, the commando training camp just outside Salisbury, to begin the nineteen-week course.

From what I can judge so far, training is excellent and differs greatly from that of the Marines. Discipline is not tremendously strict. The sergeant and corporals conducting the training seem mild compared to those at Quantico. Long hair is permitted, if it is neat, but this is necessary here to help prevent sunstroke. In spite of the moderate slackness, the training is effective and produces excellent soldiers. I believe this was due to the recruits and soldiers having a reason for serving, and a sense of mission which is presently lacking in American armed forces. The recruits volunteer because they know they are protecting the civilization built up by their immediate ancestors during the past eighty years. Rhodesia is on the defensive, which it must be, because it is really a small, weak country, a speck on the African continent, and is not a major power. One fellow from near the Mozambique border, says that the fighting is much more severe in the jungles of Mozambique than along the Zambezi river. From his home, he could often hear gunfire. Some of the recruits are as young as sixteen.

It seems peaceful and tranquil, but underneath is a sense of danger or foreboding of a possible uprising. If it were not for the army, police, and government in handling terrorists, local or from Zambia, the European culture here would vanish overnight. Nearly all the whites realize that majority rule is a folly they would never willingly accept. Only go coercion or betrayal in government would bring that about.

Life here is similar to that in the States. The only difference is the ever-present Africans. The suburbs in Salisbury are very well kept. Houses are widely spaced apart and have hedgerows surrounding the lots. There are gardens, trees, and shrubs shading the lawns. Unfortunately, I see the same decadent movies listed in the papers, and hear the same rock music on the radio.

The weather is very pleasant now, sunny, warm days and nights that often bring showers. I understand that it gets very hot in December, January, and February. Along the Zambezi, where the fighting is, it is often 120° Fahrenheit [49° Celsius] in the shade.

The people are friendly and I enjoy talking with them. I have had conversations privately with the instructors and officers, something nearly impossible in the Marines. Everyone asks me about the Marines.

It has taken me many days to write this, and I now know more than when I first began. Some of the soldiers in the army come not only from the countries listed earlier, but also from South America, Canada, and Greece. There are more Americans than I expected to find. Some, formerly with the special forces, have joined the Special Air Service (SAS), the equivalent of the Green Berets. I met one American from California who came here for the same reason I did. He was a Marine and had been severely wounded in Vietnam. He has a terrible scar on his chest. I have the opportunity to transfer to the SAS, the paratrooper battalion, and must decide on Monday, 28 March.

I am enjoying the army life so far, and I like the climate and people of Rhodesia. The Africans I have met address me as 'sir', '*bwana*', or 'boss'.

This letter covers everything I have done from the time I left home until Saturday night, 26 March. For security reasons I can't cover things in too much detail. Today we played a soccer game that turned into a free-for-all game of rugby. Very rough, but fun.

Please don't worry about me. Facilities here are excellent and modern. I believe God intended me to come here for some purpose.

Love you all very much

John.

CHAPTER 4
The Qualifying Trek for the SAS

30 April 1972

I'm on four days' leave over the weekend, and spending part of the time in Salisbury at a hotel in the downtown district. Salisbury is a very clean and neat city, and has a colonial atmosphere. Many of the buildings are only two stories with verandas running the perimeter, but this city has skyscrapers also. Across from the hotel is a park with palm and cedar trees and fountains. On the edge is a monument on the spot where in 1892 an expeditionary force, called the Pioneer Corps, relieved the besieged city during the Mashona revolt.*

Africans sweep the streets and sidewalks, and serve as porters or bellhops in the hotel. Although the shops and stores are closed for the weekend, both Africans and whites meander up and down the street, window shopping. Around the outskirts of the city are suburbs, not nearly so dense as in the States. Many houses are white stucco or brick, with gardens, hedges, shrubs and trees.

The only available church in the vicinity is St Mary's Anglican cathedral. I attended vesper services on Saturday and Sunday evenings, but skipped the morning mass.

The cathedral is a beautiful stone building, having one immense vault of an interior, with two corridors on each side, separated only by a row of towering stone pillars. Two giant circular stained-glass windows are at either end. Whites, Africans, and mulattos† attend. The service consists of organ works, choir pieces, chance by the priests, scripture readings, and hymns, but not preaching.

I applied for transfer to the Special Air Service (SAS), which is the elite airborne unit similar to the Green Berets in the US army. My application was approved, but I will not be transferred until enough people are recruited to form a new training squad. Qualification tests last for three weeks before actual training begins. I am informed they are very demanding and difficult to pass.

Last week we were introduced to a new training sergeant, a red-haired hardliner

* The Pioneer Corps in fact arrived and established Fort Salisbury in September 1890. The Mashona Rebellion took place in 1896, and was quelled by locally-formed volunteer field forces with the help of members of Imperial forces.

† In Rhodesia such persons of mixed-raced were officially known as Coloureds.

from the old school of discipline. He is an excellent instructor, very similar to those I had at Quantico, and the younger fellows are scared to death of him, fearing lest the evil, all-seeing eye fall on them.

We have two hours of drill every day – entirely different from what I had before – British style, with much more flash and finesse. Physical training is mostly sports and running. We ran two miles one day, weighed down by steel helmets, loaded packs, cartridge belts, canteens, rifles, and boots. That distance is built up to ten miles by the end of training. We play all kinds of sports: soccer, rugby, cricket, basketball, volleyball, swimming, and boxing.

The afore-mentioned sergeant told me that the army is slowly softening up, but not nearly to the extent of other Western armies, such as those of America, Sweden, and Germany. Perhaps I may have the opportunity to keep up the high training standards later on. There are many fine soldiers who have made the commandos the best bush fighters in the world. They have continually kept on top of terrorist activities and show no mercy.

The heaviest fighting is in Moçambique, and has been fairly light along the Zambezi. The papers report one South African policeman killed and several others wounded by a landmine explosion near the Caprivi Strip in South West Africa, relatively close to Rhodesia's north-west. This is the type of activity constantly occurring at the borders. The army and police have their work cut out for them, and if they were not so efficient, southern Africa would soon be a bloodbath. Whites and many Africans recognise the communist threat behind the terrorist activities, and the consequences of majority rule, yet very few are aware of the international conspiracy. The big businesses in Salisbury are run by them.

In town one sees the same pornographic movies* listed, and hear the same in rock and pop music played as in the States, but the moral fabric has not yet been eaten away so badly. 'Mod' styles have just recently been introduced.

Being in the army of a small country has its disadvantages. The food is the worst I have ever eaten, half-cooked ham, wormy apples, and slop drowned in greasy gravy. Money is taken from your pay to cover the cost, and we must buy milk and orange juice as extras, when available. Fresh vegetables are unheard of. We are

* Rhodesia had a very strict and active Board of Censors, which prohibited the screening of any movie with scenes of any form of nudity and pornography.

issued crude rifle-cleaning equipment and no solvent, but we are taught to clean the weapons sufficiently with sand, which is just as well, for when we are in the bush.

We get only two changes of fatigues and underwear, but managed to keep one pair of fatigues clean for the next morning's inspection. On the whole though, I find my lot satisfactory, and believe things will improve once I become fully adjusted to this country.

It is autumn here now, and nights are chilly, damp, and rainy, but the days are mostly sunny and warm. Mosquitoes are bad, particularly in the bush where, I'm told, tsetse flies torment you also. Windows and doors are left open without screens, but mesh netting is provided to cover beds so one can sleep. There is no central heating as we have at home. The climate is comfortable and invigorating

14 April 1972

I haven't written for two weeks because I have been undergoing selection qualification for this unit. From 7–13 April, fifteen soldiers and recruits, me among them, went marching through the mountainous wilderness of Rhodes Inyanga National Park near the Mozambique border. Parts were rocky bush country, and other parts were similar in terrain to the high Allegheny, Appalachian, or Catskill mountains, and was some of the loveliest, most picturesque country I have ever seen. The breeze was cool and the sun warm and bright, intensifying the green, white, and brown of grassy vegetation and scrub forest growth, interspersed with grey and black outcroppings of rock. Crystal-clear streams gushed forth and tumbled down through the valleys, and one could drink this water without fear of pollution. Palm-like trees bordering the streams reminded me of Eden. On the mountain peaks one could see for miles over green and brown valleys, and the plains to the west. Large areas were cultivated in pine and fir. This is the best way to see Africa, as Stanley and Livingstone and other explorers must have seen it; the Africa the tourist misses.

We had to march an average of thirteen miles per day through that country for five days straight, carrying thirty-pound packs, rifles, food rations for a three-day supply, and using map and compass to find our way. Only five of the sixteen completed all five legs of the journey. Some were injured in the rugged terrain, one caught malaria, and the others were just too exhausted to continue.

We were dropped off along a road, singly or in pairs, to make our way to predetermined rendezvous points at fixed times. We travelled up and down treacherous mountains, swampy valleys, and grassy *gomos*, or rocky hills.

I saw first-hand how the Africans live, away from European influence: barely scratching out an existence on grubby little farms, with round, one-room, thatched-roof huts, and with chickens and naked children romping in the dust and filth. Some allow their long-horned cattle to graze the earth bare.

The first night my partner and I spent in the stone foundation of a long abandoned *kraal*, or hut, which had four big trees sprouting from it, sheltering us from the cold, damp winds.

The next morning, Sunday, we spotted deer-like antelope on the grassy plateau, and could hear baboons barking from the nearby rocky mountains. Later we crossed one of the many narrow, deep, swift, and treacherous rivers, and, just above the first rendezvous point, we faced a magnificent waterfall. We were twelve hours late, and my partner quit from exhaustion.

I continued north, and after getting lost twice, managed to get to a small town at the foot of the second objective, a peak on top of a gigantic mountain called World's View. I could not find the trail up, and because darkness was setting in, spent the night in the British South African Police (BSAP) station in the town. After I had bathed and eaten, a young police officer invited me to his home. He is the son of Austrian immigrants, who came to the country in the early 1950s. We talked about Rhodesia, the States, big-game hunting, terrorist activity, and the communists behind it (of which Rhodesians are very much aware), and even the role played by the World Council of Churches.

The next morning, Monday, I started up the mountain, followed by a police dog, a black and tan Doberman that stayed with me all day. I followed a trail, passing a pioneer cemetery and an African village, and soon after proceeded straight up the face, made up of three progressively steeper and higher mountains. I spotted a troop of baboons on the second. Small, young ones scampered and chased one another over the rocks, and older ones barked and screamed, protesting the intrusion of the dog and me into their private domain.

The top was alpine-like, with club mosses and grassy, round knolls, crossed by small streams. We also came across some ancient stone-walled ruins. We later found a road that led to the highest precipice, but the difficult climb was well worth the spectacular view. Returning down the road, I found two others of the company, one with a badly sprained ankle, the other just exhausted. Later the SAS sergeant picked us all up, but was angry because he had to drive all the way back to the police station to return the dog. He asked, "Did the dog show you the way up?"

The next day there was a fifteen-mile speed march, initiated by a gruelling climb up another steep mountain, followed by too many other hills to remember. This was a killer, and only six of the sixteen made the march in the required time of six hours.

The last day, Wednesday, brought the last five of us together. The morning was foggy, and mist obscured all the landmarks which were to guide us. We could go only by compass bearings alone, over grassy *gomos* so difficult to climb, and vegetation so profuse, that it was nearly impossible to get through. The mists cleared later in the morning, and we passed through dense stands of hardwood trees and plantations of Scotch pine, and climbed up the last mountain to a fire tower. From there through more pine forests, with thick beds of needles to cushion our sore feet. We passed a sawmill on the way to an intersection near a small village called Juliasdale. I had to march alone an additional eight miles to the base camp, to make up for a leg I missed earlier. The ordeal was over.

I can only attribute my success to the willpower God gave me to keep walking. I was not up to the exertion physically, and many times I gave up hope when at my wits end as to where I was. At times the agony of walking over rocky ground, with my pack cutting into my shoulders, nearly drove me mad. Something besides my own determination kept me going. The day after our return to Salisbury, the officer-in-charge spoke to each of us. He told me, "Coey, I don't know how the hell you got through it all, but you have the guts and determination to carry you through."

I will be with the SAS for the next six months in training; the selection, I hear, is the worst part. This unit is the elite; the finer elements are in it, and accommodation and food are much better than at the commando training camp. We have more free time, and I am resting up over the weekend.

Since there are only five of us to begin a new SAS training squad, we will be trained to drive military vehicles and Land Rovers for the next week or two until more trainees are recruited.

I have now spoken with soldiers and recruits from all over southern Africa, and they understand the absurdity of communist rule. If it comes, it will only be the result of capitulation by the government to the conspiracy. I anticipate the European civilization here collapsing very quickly should the pincer movement of communist takeover be fully exploited.

I have received a letter from S.E.D. Brown, who is requesting permission to reprint my 'protest' in his journal, but suggesting that I leave out any references to Rhodesia, since that would make me 'a marked man' by 'the liberals who abound in Rhodesia'. I sent a telegram back telling him to print the letter as it is.

22 April 1972

I'm overjoyed that S.E.D. Brown is going to reprint my 'protest'. Apart from that, things have been rather dull at camp since I finished the episode in the mountains. The days since then have been pleasant and leisurely, and will continue that way until regular training commences again in the middle of May.

CHAPTER 5
Rhodesian Autumn of 1972

22 April 1972

Driving the Land Rovers is easy, once you get used to the clutch. Getting used to the roads is another matter; driving customs are just the opposite from those in the States. Rhodesians use the left side of the road, and everybody drives like a madman. We take forty-five minutes off for tea at ten in the morning, and an hour off after lunch to doze – typical of the leisurely, slower-paced life over here. Our weekends are free, and we often go into Salisbury on Saturday mornings to do business and to buy extra provisions. The remainder of the weekend I write, swim, or run in the afternoons, or just rest up. There are now chapel services at 10:30 Sundays. So I'll be going to these.

Most of the fighting in the Zambezi valley is done by the commando units, and is not very heavy. The SAS is not very active now either, but rumours circulate about their raids. A while back, a train loaded with communist-supplied ammunition was blown up in Zambia. Official sources claim it was due to accident, but more than likely the SAS did it. The nature of SAS activity is secretive, and security is strict. So very little of what is done is ever reported, or even known by all the members of the squadron.

I enquired about getting a Luger 9mm pistol this morning. Gun registration is strict, and I can only get one with the permission of the officer commanding, provided I have a good reason for getting one.

I am only the third American to join the SAS, although there are others in the commando battalions. The first, I hear, deserted and went back to the States. The other, from California, is still here, but I seldom ever get a chance to speak with him.

Please send a small American flag, 18 inch by 24 inch, or about that size. We are fixing up the barrack room with flags of the countries of our origin.

30 April 1972

This past week has been more interesting. I'm still on the drivers' course, but this gives me the opportunity to see the territory around Salisbury, as well as the city itself. On Monday and Tuesday we drove west of town to an army training centre called Domboshawa to participate in attack exercises. On the way there we passed areas like Ohio farmland; gentle, rolling hills, cultivated in corn and pasture. The cattle are unbelievable; lean, gaunt Texas longhorns* seem to do best in the wild vegetation, and are followed by snowy-white cattle egrets.

Domboshawa is rugged, rocky, hill country, covered in scrub bush. The first night, one of the selectees and I were posted on separate hilltop observation posts, and we fired flares periodically to indicate our positions. The other three and a sergeant set up a basecamp in a nearby village. Sixteen members of another training troop had to bypass the observation posts and reach camp without being seen or heard. I spotted three, and bombarded them with smoke grenades.

Both that night and the next were the loveliest I have seen. A brilliant, nearly full moon illuminated the area in silvery whiteness. Stars filled a crystal-clear sky, and you could hear the longhorn cattle low and bellow a far way off, night birds whistling as they captured insect, and crickets chirping as on a summer evening at home.

The next night was more exciting. The 'mighty five'. and our sergeant set up at the basecamp, and prepared for an assault by the other training group. The camp was bordered on one side by a row of huge rocks and on the other by thick brush, concealing our position. A stream flowed a short distance beyond.

We set up a perimeter of barbed wire and trip flares, and positioned ourselves at strategic spots covering avenues of attack. We had one machine gun, and each had a semi-automatic rifle, as well as flares and smoke grenades. The attack was to come between 1930 hours and midnight. As we waited and watched, we heated coffee and roasted sausages called *boerewors*. Midnight passed without the attack taking place.

The night chill was penetrating, and the shadows created illusions, as our anxiety and grogginess increased. Finally, the moon set behind a hill at about 0400 hours, casting the valley into darkness. The attackers swarmed over the stream bank and into the barbed wire and trip flares. The battle site lit up, with flares and thunder flashes [like very large firecrackers] that made very loud noises, bright flashes, and much smoke. We blasted each other with blanks as the camp was overrun.

* Texas longhorns were not found in Rhodesia, so these would have been one of the indigenous breeds.

The battle was over in five minutes. I don't think anyone would have survived if we had used live ammunition, because many of the weapons jammed after firing only a few rounds. We use standard NATO weapons,* inferior to those used in the United States. We returned to barracks later that morning and got some much-needed sleep.

We continued with driving for the rest of the week, running errands and delivering messages for officers around Salisbury, but this took us to many interesting places.

I received a letter from S.E.D. Brown saying that he would reprint my 'protest' in the May edition of the *South African Observer.* I was glad to hear from Congressman John Schmitz, and I would be happy to inform him of terrorist activity over here. I don't expect any of the congressmen will use my 'protest'.

Mr Brown sent me the March and April issues of the *South African Observer*; it is good to read from a reliable news source again, concerning Rhodesian prime minister Ian Smith and his government's activities. It appears that Smith is no more of a statesman than Richard Nixon. Also, Smith's twenty-two year-old son was arrested a while back for possessing drugs.

The Rhodesians are for the most part anti-communist, but ignorance of the international forces, I fear, will prove the demise of the European civilization. The moral corruption of Europe and America is making headway year also.

That's about all to report this week. The food is great now and I have regained my lost weight. I wish you could send me one thing – my Marine Corps cap. All the blokes want to see it.

7 May 1972

This weekend I'm on telephone and guard duty, which amounts to sitting in the guard room and waiting for an occasional call.

This week a new batch of recruits arrived for pre-selection training. In two weeks they will have to go through what I did. At least six of the nineteen that arrived must make it so that there would be enough people to start a new training course. I'm getting tired of waiting.

Morality in the forces is about as good as one can expect for an army. Drinking

* The weapon referred to here is the 7.62mm FN FAL rifle, issued to all branches of the Rhodesian defence forces.

and fighting are the major off-duty preoccupations, and most of the fellows and girls seem rather loose, which may be good or bad, depending on your viewpoint. The Rhodesians are not really a religious people, but are more inclined to sports – horse- and auto-racing, and rugby and soccer; but, and like Americans, these people participate in their own team sport, rather than just spectate. There are all kinds in the army, but most seem decent. They are really no different from the people I met while at Quantico, and are probably little different from those in any military force.

When out in the bush one has to be careful where you sit or step, because there are many more poisonous snakes and spiders then in the States. In fact, nearly anything that crawls or creeps may sting or bite. They are giant centipedes and scorpions, and tsetse flies in some parts. We have to take malaria pills twice a week because mosquitoes swarm at night. There is little chance of a snake bite but, if you are bitten, not much can be done. The poison paralyzes your nervous system, and your heart and lungs stop functioning.*

There is a drug problem in Rhodesia, but less than in America. Long hair and the hippy syndrome came to this country just three years ago, but appears to be making rapid progress in the youth I see on the streets of Salisbury. Rhodesia has a draft policy such that every boy is conscripted at age eighteen, or when he completes high school. He is trained for nine months in a territorial force, after which he can then leave or continue to serve in the RLI or SAS, if he makes it. Even though drug addicts may be drafted into the army by this method, most are weeded out in the first nine months. All the main regular fighting units – such as the RLI and SAS – are entirely volunteer, since no-one is forced to serve after nine months' service† This would be a good policy for the USA, I think.

I found out why the Rhodesian SAS is designated 'C' squadron. There are only two others. 'A' squadron in Britain (where the SAS was first conceived by David

* This would depend on the type of venomous snake. There are two main groups of venom: neurotoxic, which is what John is referring to, for example cobras. The other group is haemolytic, which affects the blood system and tissues, which includes the adders. Snakebite serum was normally always available, and fatalities amongst troops were extremely rare, if at all.

† Such territorial troops, however, were called-up for periodic tours of duty every year thereafter.

Stirling during World War II) and 'B' squadron in New Zealand.* Each is an autonomous force within its respective country.

13 May 1972

Last weekend my one day of phone and guard duty was extended over Sunday, and I got some funny phone calls. The father of one of the new recruits called. Thinking I was one of the training officers, he proceeded to tell me what a cheeky fellow his son is, and how he hopes the army will straighten him out. I assured him the army will.

Two new blokes joined us on Monday. One is a South African from Durban, formerly of the merchant marine and the South African paratroopers. He is a good fellow, but is something of a pirate and mercenary. The other fellow is a Dutchman from Amsterdam, formerly in the Netherlands air force. He is thirty-one and well educated. But he decided to forgo the SAS and joined the RLI instead.

On Wednesday morning we drove on from Umtali to the resort of Hot Springs, and then to the Birchenough Bridge. Hot Springs is a resort of interest only because geothermal water seeps to the earth's surface. But the bridge is worth seeing, because it is a single, huge arch of steel over the Sabi River. Perhaps one of the largest such spans in the world, the bridge is suspended from giant cables.

The Sabi River is broad and shallow, about the size of the Ohio River, and is reported to be inhabited by crocs and hippos in places. As we drove through the Eastern Highlands, the scenery was spectacular: green with scrub brush, though rocky and sparse in places. Near the Sabi the land is eroded and barren from overgrazing by African cattle. Grotesque baobab trees are common. They have an immense base, some fifteen to twenty feet in diameter. The younger trees narrow to a pointed top about twenty feet high, giving the trunk a carrot shape. [The older, much larger trees don't have this shape, but have a massive uniform girth, topped by a mass of branches resembling roots, almost as if it is upside down.]

We returned by the same route out of the highlands, through the green, rich, and fertile grassy veld land to Salisbury.

Thursday and Friday were not so nice. Written and oral driver examinations and

* This can be confusing, as the British SAS is in fact made up of A, B, C, D, E and G squadrons. The New Zealand SAS has A, B, C, D, E and Support squadrons

then spent the rest of the days washing and cleaning vehicles. This is the dirtiest, most miserable job in the army, removing grease and dirt from the engines, undercarriages and exteriors of trucks and Land Rovers.

We all got into trouble for not saluting officers properly. So all of us are on guard duty this weekend for 'lack of discipline'. The colour sergeant threatens that we will have to go through selection twice if we get into trouble again.

I heard a news report that a blockade and effective bombing have commenced this past week in Vietnam. The war could have been won years ago if similar action had been taken sooner. The past two administrations are responsible for the deaths of thousands of Americans and Vietnamese, and should be tried for treason and war crimes.

In another newsflash last Friday, I heard that someone was warning Rhodesians not to fall prey to financier and big banking interests, as has so much of Europe and America. He declared that these interests were responsible for the Russian and communist revolutions everywhere in the world since 1917, and pose the greatest threat to Rhodesia. Ah, yes, the conspiracy is closing in on Rhodesia. We hear news reports of increased terrorist activity in Angola and Mozambique. We don't hear much about trouble in Rhodesia, even in the army, and we can't talk about what is heard.

These past few weeks have been pleasant, but in two weeks we go back to the hard business of soldiering.

CHAPTER 6
Overseeing the New Recruits at World's View

29 May 1972

I could not write last weekend because I went on another selection course at Rhodes Inyanga National Park. I did not undergo the ordeal again, but helped supervise another group doing the same as I did last month. This really turned out to be a sort of a vacation, for I returned to see the places which I marched in during selection. This time I went by vehicle, allowing me to take some valuable pictures.

About twenty-two recruits were dropped in the bush to start their five days of marching.

Monday morning I rode up the Inyanga mountains to World's View and took photographs of the countryside and the blokes marching on. Three had dropped out the day before, and one had strained his neck when he tumbled down a steep hill.

At about 1900 hours, two of the recruits on selection suddenly arrived at camp. After they had made their way to the day's rendezvous, some civilians drove by their camp and offered to take them to the local inn to get 'water'. While the two were inside, the 'civvies' drove off, leaving them. The recruits then walked to our camp where they had some explaining to do. They were ordered to walk back to the rendezvous and to carry two seven-pound bricks in their packs the next day. This was too much for one of them and he dropped out.

I walked down the road at about 2000 hours. The moon illuminated the surrounding *gomos* and mountains, and I could see the silhouette of the Inyanga mountains to the north. Overhead was the Southern Cross, which reminds the Southern Hemisphere of the sacrifice of Christ, just as the constellation Cygnus, the swan, or Northern Cross, reminds the Northern Hemisphere.

Tuesday was a glorious day. I carried on an American tradition originated by Stanley on his journeys down the Nile and over the Congo River do the Atlantic. Wearing my pith helmet, I climbed the highest mountain in Rhodesia, Inyangani, carrying the American flag to the top. Then I finished the journey over nineteen miles of *gomos* bordering the Pungwe River and gorge.

The morning was cold and misty, but it cleared with the rising of the sun to make for a brilliant day. It was time for the gruelling speed march for the blokes on selection, and I was assigned to encourage stragglers to continue the march and not to give up. I succeeded in getting four to complete it, two just barely in time, by forcing them into a dramatic sprint over the last three-quarters of a mile, after which both collapsed. It gives me a good feeling to know that I help them succeed when, otherwise, they would not have made it.

The scenery on the march was truly spectacular. Along one stretch overlooking Pungwe gorge one could see into Mozambique. The mountains are covered in veld grass, but capped in nearly vertical rock outcroppings. Fountains cascaded over the steep canyon walls to a valley floor blanketed in jungle. Down the other side of the ridge from the road was another grassy valley with a trout stream meandering through it, and with occasional fern trees along its banks. The region is a veritable Eden, certainly a tribute to the handiwork of God, and evidence of creation. For never could such a paradise happen by chance.

On Tuesday the army and police got word to prepare for riots, pending the government's decision concerning the Pearce Commission.* The decision was an unqualified 'no compromise' with the British, but no trouble developed. I believe the resumption of sanctions will be better for Rhodesia, forcing the country to become self-sufficient. No-one was satisfied with the compromise: the communists, because the European civilization would not be surrendered fast enough; the right, because the civilization would eventually be surrendered.

Wednesday was our last full day at Inyanga. I rode with the officers to a fire tower overlooking hundreds of acres of pine plantations which form a patchwork of deep green carpet over the mountains. The Scots pines grow three feet per year, six feet in some of the valleys, and all are planted in rows for easy thinning and harvesting. The layer of pine needles on the forest floor is two feet thick, and quite a relief for sore, tired feet.

As we marvelled at the landscape, the recruits trudged slowly up to the top, one by one, haggard, nearly exhausted, and gingerly stepping on sore, swollen, blistered, and even bloody feet. This is really an inspiration to see: youth with guts

* The Pearce Commission was instituted by the British government to ascertain directly from all sectors of Rhodesia's population whether or not the proposals for a settlement, agreed on 21 November 1972, were acceptable. In May 1972, the commission's report was tabled in the British House of Commons, their findings clearly spelling out that the majority of Rhodesians rejected the proposals.

– a contrast to the hippies and weaklings one sees in town and the universities, although the recruits come from those same places also.

Driving back to camp, we spotted a falcon perched on a utility pole. Hastily we set up a net trap baited with a small chick. No sooner had we set the trap and left, than the falcon swooped into the net and was snared. It is a beautiful bird – fierce, defiant, hissing and spitting. The lieutenant will train it to hunt rabbits.

Later that afternoon the troops came back to camp, dog-tired, but showing pride and satisfaction.

I developed a strong friendship with a South African chap from Durban, and we had a long talk on Wednesday night. He had not only been in the merchant marine and the crack south African paratroop regiment, the Parabats, but he had also been in the French Foreign Legion and with the mercenaries in the Congo. He fought for Moise Tshombe, who said he was a CIA puppet, but later resisted the conspiracy. Tshombe was later done away with by an alleged heart attack. My new friend told me he nearly killed a sergeant when he was in the Foreign Legion. The NCO had kicked him in the face, and shortly thereafter, he deserted. He told me that he is ready to settle down after he does some service in the SAS, and that he had seen too much evil, such as nuns raped in the Congo and missionaries butchered. He hopes to run his deceased father's sugarcane farm outside Durban, where African prisoners cut cane from dawn to dusk for twenty cents a day. He gave me his old throwing knife that he bought in Germany.

That night the chaps celebrated their success with a drinking party and by singing old army songs, some at least as old as World War I, such as *Waltzing Matilda* and *Inky Dinky Parlez Vous.*

This weekend is the last easy one. We start the basic-training course next week. For the next eight weeks we will have drill, weapons training, and physical training, during which time we won't be allowed out of camp. The holidays are over for a time.

[This is a letter John wrote the same day, 29 May 1972, to his Sunday school class at St Paul's Lutheran Church, Columbus, Ohio.]

> My dear girls and boys,
>
> I hope that one day you too may come and see this wonderful country. It is a land of mountains and grassy prairies, with strange wild animals like

you see on the postcards.

I'm in the army here, for there is trouble, and the communists and terrorists are constantly trying to destroy the Christianity and way of life brought to this land by young English and German cousins, not too many years ago. As a soldier and paratrooper I will be fighting these enemies.

You boys must learn to be brave and strong, and you girls must in time raise strong, brave sons also, to fight for and defend our Christian faith. Remember that Jesus Christ is our Saviour and we do not need to fear death because he died for us.

If you obey God and His commandments, you will be happy. If you disobey God, you make things miserable for yourself and others. Keep coming to church and Sunday school and continue to bring your friends.

CHAPTER 7
SAS Recruit Course

My SAS recruit course started this week. So, once again, I go through the hard grind of drill, physical training, getting weapons and uniforms, and keeping the barracks clean, clean, clean. It all brings back memories of Quantico quite vividly.

There are fifteen in my training course now, mostly from Rhodesia, but some from South Africa, and one from Portugal. Discipline is strict.

I learn much inside information in the army, but I can't reveal anything because of security measures. I could write about terrorists' activity only at the risk of going to prison. I would be particularly suspect because of some bad experiences the government has had here with CIA agents.

Although this is a peaceful country and I am fully satisfied here, but I know the peace will not last. I think the next six months will reveal the total picture much more clearly.

Two weeks of training are done already; the time really zips by now. These first eight weeks are an intensified commando training programme; then we are taken to the Zambezi Valley for another endurance qualification, this time in skirmishing tactics.

Last Thursday and Friday I watched the band of the Rhodesian African Rifles (RAR) practising on the drill field. The band is all African, including the drum major, and the precision, finesse, and music are tremendous. There is nothing that surpasses a military band for instilling pride and *esprit de corps*. One must admire these Africans in the RAR. They are superb soldiers, and they do a magnificent job fighting terrorists.

I am subscribing to the monthly journal *Property and Finance*. It is much like the *South Africa Observer*, but is more business oriented. It is very critical of the Smith government and uncovers much corruption and the influence of international finance.

I am glad that the US Congress voted not to renew the embargo on Rhodesian chrome.

Last week I was asked in a letter whether I am still happy in what I am doing. I replied that I have never been more satisfied than now, knowing that I opposed the aliens in the United States government, and that I am playing a small role in the conflict between the West and Satan's conspiracy. I am happy to be learning ways necessary to fight for our freedom. But, most of all, I am helping to unify the Europeans, simply by my presence and association with these people. For they are coming to realize that there is no important difference between Americans, white Africans or Europeans. The accents, dialects, and languages are superficial. The customs, religion, styles of government, and thinking are the same. I believe that only when all European peoples are unified can communism and the alien conspiracy be smashed.

18 June 1972

Training is moving on rapidly. We have had squad movements, fire-control orders, and simulated ambushing, such as was used in Europe in the last war, but it is not really useful in African bush country. It is taught, anyway, as basics. I have learned how difficult it is to spot a well-hidden enemy, and how easy it is to get killed. It is interesting that trench warfare is still taught in the RLI. Sometimes we have practised bayonet fighting – still used even now – although to a lesser extent that in the 17th–19th centuries. Use of the bayonet is not stressed nearly so much as in the US army or Marines. Friday we were taught to stalk and to move silently. It is the same method perfected during the Indian wars, but will be used again, I'm sure.

Because of sloppy order in the barracks, we stand for 'shine parades' several times during the week. This is an evening inspection when everything must be spotless: floors polished, windows cleaned, lockers perfectly straightened, beds made in hospital manner, and men dressed in drill order.

There is an American that joined the RLI a few weeks ago. He is from Florida and is somewhat fat. He refused to run when ordered to do so by an officer, and was put in detention barracks by the military police. There he was stripped of his clothes, soaked with water, and left without food in his cold cell – until he started running when ordered. The next day he was running very fast. Such is life in the army.

Some revealing facts concerning the SAS have come to light. It may once have been an elite force of self-disciplined specialists trained in unconventional warfare, but now its spirit is broken. It is deteriorating and resting on the laurels of the past. Permissiveness and laxness in discipline have undermined the squadron's immediate effectiveness. Some of the best NCOs have been broken with despair because some of the officers in command are more interested in social life than in soldiering. Many of the troopers are drunkards, and wild drinking parties carry on several nights each week. Most of the 'soldiers' being recruited are 16- or 17-year-old kids, and they remain quite immature despite training which, I am glad to say, is still excellent.

My general impression is that the SAS has tremendous potential, considering the human resources in it, but I fear a catastrophe should the unit be thrust into a major war. I believe, as a corporal suggested, that a good operation would do much to restore morale and *esprit de corps.* He told me that there are three types that join the army: the young kids who cannot find any other work; the highly educated and well-off, looking for adventure, excitement, or a break from the old life; and the professional, who joins for action and the opportunity to fight the enemy. God grant us more of the last.

25 June 1972

There are some more interesting things to disclose. A corporal was telling me of some American friends of his who were willing to set up business here, but were turned down by the government. This same government grants monopolies, and the resultant shoddy products are blamed on the 'sanctions', but not on a lack of competition. Hmmm. This fellow is pretty much disgruntled with the army and Rhodesia in particular. He came from Zambia, and will soon leave the army; his open criticisms may well be inaccurate.

A close friend and I have 'jumped the fence' and attended services at a nearby Baptist church, since no-one seems to know when base chapel services are held. We don't have to be sneaky now, and we have met some very nice people who have invited us to their homes. The change of atmosphere from camp to church is a real relief. The people are certainly devout Christians, and at least are opposed to the World Council of Churches. One member commented, "John, you are here to stay"? He may be right.

Sunday after church my buddy and I were invited out to the Baptist Mission Society headquarters for dinner by a husband and wife team from Alberta, Canada. This is the main mission centre for Rhodesia and Zambia, and houses the missionary families when they are not in the bush. Several families are American and Canadian. Facilities are really modern compared to the thatched huts they use in the bush.

I was told that the mission work is going satisfactorily amongst the Africans, although some missions were abandoned because of terrorist activity in the Zambezi Valley. Also, all whites are in constant jeopardy in Zambia. Black nationalists in that country demand that the missionaries give all or get out, and stir up resistance to Christian teachings. The brother of the Canadian missionary had been premier of Alberta, but was ousted in a recent election, thanks partly to Pierre Trudeau, for whom they have no use.

I was introduced to an old British soldier, a major, who was a relic of the bygone empire and a former administrator in India for twenty years during and after World War I. India, he said, was ruled by autonomous provinces of ethnic groups such as Parsees, Hindus and Muslims. Most of the trouble came from the African religions and the caste system.

Late that afternoon I attended a Bible study group that was really a 'bull session', in which everyone professed his interpretation of the scriptures.

Some of the people I met today are at least aware that the West is declining and dying – in Europe, America, even southern Africa – and they attribute it to the rejection of Christianity.

Five weeks are completed now. One more, and the worst will be over. This is about the equivalent of my six weeks at Quantico.

Next weekend is a holiday; Rhodes and Founders, a four-day weekend commemorating the founding of Rhodesia in 1895.* I couldn't get a reservation at Victoria Falls, so I will spend that weekend with a friend in Bulawayo.

I received a reply from Congressman Clarence Miller, and I was really happy to read what he has thought my 'protest', and that at least some good will come of it. My mates never cease to marvel that I get letters from the US Congress.

The bus strike continues in Salisbury. It was prompted by the African National Council (ANC), a communist-front group. So the conspiracy is at work here also.

I spoke with a recruit from Belgium. He says Europe is so crowded and sick of socialism, that thousands have left Britain, France, Italy, and other countries. Most

* The founding date of the country is 13 September 1890, when the Pioneer Column held a full-dress parade and service to commemorate their arrival the previous day. The site was named Fort Salisbury, after the then British prime minister the 3rd Marquess of Salisbury. The holiday was introduced in 1920.

go to South Africa, and from there, many filter north to Rhodesia.

In town this morning I met two old buddies from my original RLI training troop. They have just completed their fourteen-week recruit course; never have I seen such an improvement in appearance. When I first met them, they were fat and sloppy, and had long greasy hair. Now they are lean and hard, well-groomed and neat, but most importantly, trained soldiers.

War seems inevitable now: in Mozambique, in the Zambezi Valley, or perhaps in a Third Conflagration. The barbarians and other enemies of the West will never rest until they destroy our civilization and way of life. Even if we choose not, they will wage war on us.

The time of peace in southern Africa is quickly running out, and the fate and destiny of European civilization here will soon be manifest. The struggle and conflict will take

thousands of lives and, most likely, I will be amongst them. I only pray that I may help win the victory for all Western people.

I have represented America well in selection, in training, and in the episode with the flag in May. The people I have met here respect the Americans more when they hear what I have done. I am pleased that some of the young people at church have also been inspired. God has given me the chance to do more for my country by coming here than I ever did in all the years back home.

CHAPTER 8
Tactics and Manoeuvres

Training has been intensive and will get tougher over the next six weeks, as we get into tactics and manoeuvres, the basics of all infantry.

Last weekend I went to the town of Bulawayo, a very clean city, even more clean than Salisbury. It is in south-west Rhodesia, and a five-hour drive from the capital. I stayed at the home of my best friend, George Jenkinson, who is training with me and will go on the officers' course next year. His family, like others I have met, extended the most gracious hospitality I have ever experienced.

From Saturday to Monday we camped out at the Rhodes Matopos National Park where Cecil Rhodes is buried. This is magnificent country: sparse, dry, rocky with rugged hills vegetated in scrub brush. It reminds me of Arizona and New Mexico, and, like those areas, it is a major cattle-producing region of this country.

It is so easy to slip back to being a civilian, and I quickly did so during those four days. It was so good to spend some time with a Christian family, and very difficult to snap back to the training routine again last Wednesday. I had the chance to see other towns, such as Gwelo (where I will train next January), Que Que and Gatooma. The country around these places is most what one thinks of as typical Africa: grassy veld with flat-crown and crooked trees.

One can easily lose contact with the outside world when he is forced to concentrate solely on military subjects. There is hardly any time to read the newspapers and periodicals I get.

Rhodesians generally still respect America, but they can't understand why it is fighting communism in Vietnam but supports it in southern Africa. Most think it is just misunderstanding and do not believe me when I tell them the United States is ruled by a pro-communist, anti-Western oligarchy. But at least they listen.

The training officers are tightening up on discipline for recruits. Inspections are getting to become like those in the RLI, and there is a crackdown on slackness. I was confined to the barracks for having a sloppy locker during inspection. Discipline is desirable until applied to oneself. It is all for the best, however. The squadron could stand an overhaul.

The sergeant says there is only one SAS, even though 'A', 'B', and 'C' squadrons are of different armies and countries. The SAS was formed in 1941 in Britain with 'A' and 'B' squadrons. The Rhodesian 'C' Squadron SAS has its origins in the Malayan Emergency of the early 1950s, when it was initially also referred to as the Malaya Scouts. I think it is a good unit to stay with.

Today was spent on the range firing the FN rifle and machine gun.* My firing was so poor that an officer commented, "Well, Coey, at least you're consistent."

About two months ago I told one of my mates that he ought to forget the civilian life, particularly women, to be an effective soldier. Now I find myself thinking of a certain girl to the point of distraction, and it is difficult to concentrate on military subjects.

This evening we practised night fighting – creeping up on an objective in darkness without being seen or heard. It was an excellent experience.

24 July 1972

The course just suffered the most difficult week of training thus far. The weeding-out process is on, but everyone manages to survive the pressure applied: shine parades every night, confinement to barracks, extra duties, and always the quips and wisecracks during drill. The course failed the inspection by the OC (officer commanding), resulting in CB (confined to barracks) being threatened for a month. Much difficulty arises from the inability of the course to work as a team. There is some teamwork and cooperation, but each man is for himself first and foremost.

I am proud to be going through all this, for I will be more of a man for it, and I would want my son to go through the same. One's former pride is shattered by the humiliation of scrubbing floors, cleaning filth, removing cigarette butts, digging ditches, and other grovelling. But the humiliation is replaced by a new pride in having endured a difficult time and coming through.

26 July 1972

Today the course did a compass-reconnaissance march at Domboshawa. On the march we passed several ancient gravesites that had all the inscriptions obliterated. They are made of stone with crosses on top. Probably some pioneers are buried

* The machine gun John refers to is the standard 7.62mm MAG (*Mitrailleuse d'Appui Général*) light machine gun used by all branches of the Rhodesian armed forces.

there, but I kept wondering:

who were they? What did they think? What did they do?

Domboshawa is a dry, rocky, desolate area, but beautiful cattle country. It is a Tribal Trust Land (TTL), and African villages and *kraals* are common.*

As we walked past a mission school, black children flocked to the fence and waved at us. For these we fight too. Without the white man they can never have peace.

Life in the army is an experience under total tyranny. All of one's time is at the disposal of the military. Although we are given time off, the plans and dates we make must too often be broken. Freedom of speech and writing is severly limited for security reasons. Recruits particularly must jump and obey every silly whim of stupid corporals and sergeants that exploit their bit of authority to the hilt.

I can only say that I gave up my freedom for the sake of my family, families like mine, and the freedom of my people. My mates think I'm crazy for passing up good paying jobs in forestry or some other field, and volunteering for this wretched existence. But the experience is invaluable and will pay off in the long run. It will bring me to my destiny and life-purpose.

Today I watched the passing-out parade of the recruit course just ahead of mine. The minister of defence spoke dryly of how the SAS will be ready if Rhodesia is attacked from the borders or from within its midst. However, always the great threat is ignored: subversion and sell-out in government.

31 July 1972

Only a few more weeks and basics will be over.

I have met a girl, the daughter of Canadian missionaries. She is a close friend of mine, but in September she will be going to St Paul, Minnesota, to attend nursing school. She and her parents are not fully convinced that a conspiracy exists, but they know things are not right.

3 August 1972

Training now is comparable to that of the Special Forces, and we are really getting tough. Last Monday we ran carrying logs in three-man teams. Wednesday we

* These TTLs were in effect reserves set aside for the exclusive habitation by indigenous black Rhodesians. *Kraal* is in fact the more commonly word used for an African village.

completed a fifteen-mile speed march in three hours. We carried twenty-five-pound packs and rifles, and alternated walking and running. A young bull sent three chaps howling and climbing up a tree. Thursday, just to follow up, we did a compass march. I've never been in better physical condition.

Shine parades occur every night. The sergeant screams at us, "If you want to be professional soldiers, you must meet army standards, pay attention to detail, and discipline." He always finds something wrong. He tells us to be ready at nine o'clock, and doesn't come until ten-fifteen. Meanwhile, we just stand on tired, bruised feet, waiting while the sergeant drinks. But we learn discipline.

I know that all this is to test and to prepare me for ordeals to come. The evil I suffer now will prepare me to resist a worse evil ahead. I no longer feel any animosity towards the training personnel who harass and antagonize us so much. I can take anything now.

God is the Supreme Commander whose intelligence is without flaw. His orders and mission for each of us must be obeyed and never questioned. Though we are separated from our dearest, there is always the rendezvous when our battles are over. May God grant us success.

Although one could find many faults in this army, the training is the very best. I am fortunate to be on this course because it has really been upgraded over the past several weeks. This is quite a contrast to trends in most armies.

We have skirmishing, unarmed combat, tactics, and training in all weapons. I am now a marksman with the sub-machine gun.

Early August 1972

[first part censored] … base camp on one side of the river and scouted the enemy position on the other at night. Entirely too much noise is made. Something made me sick in my stomach, and on reaching the last rendezvous, I vomited severely. Somehow I just can't get enthusiastic about all this, and just don't care. But I know I must go through to the end. The other night I dreamed I returned home after getting out of the army. I wanted to rejoin. I missed it so much. I will carry on.

10 August 1972

I visited a friend of mine last night and attended a Bible-study session with her. It was conducted by an extremely intelligent American missionary. These Christians seem so concerned about the second coming of Christ, and how much prophecy has or has not been fulfilled. They have fallen for the myth that the expansion of Israel is preordained by God.

At drill this morning our weekend passes were cancelled because we made mistakes. The only point in doing this is to harass and pressure us to see who can't take it. Thank God there are only two more weeks of it.

13 August 1972

I still do not regret coming here. It has been the experience of a lifetime, full of purpose and meaning, and has provided the chance for me to stand up for my beliefs. I was intended to do these things, and few people are better suited for them. I will have to eventually break with the Rhodesian government also. No politician can be trusted, and all seem to succumb to the conspiracy. Smith's government may try to set up majority rule, and some of his people are rabid about it. The University of Rhodesia is no better than Ohio State University in third-rate liberal and Marxist teaching. I believe that I must stay in the army and go through the officers' training, for I may then be a position to help save the situation when the time comes. I feel I'm being prepared for something, just what I do not know.

I was told by our training officer that I am one of the best recruits they have and stand a good chance of winning a recruit-of-the-year award.

CHAPTER 9
Torture and Spring Training

This last week has been one to remember. Monday and Tuesday were spent on observation operations at the Mazoe Dam near Salisbury. Everything was going perfectly. We had to march into a given area and locate and observe an 'enemy' camp without being detected. But on the last day we left too late. A second party came into our camp and gave away our position. The 'enemy' surrounded us, and seven were captured and taken away for interrogation by torture.

Two had to kneel on branches while holding big rocks over their heads. The rest of us were strung up to trees by our thumbs, leaving us on tiptoes, our arms extended behind our backs, and bodies bent over like jack knives. The pain was excruciating, but to make matters worse, our caps were pulled down, tied over our faces, and saturated with water, such that we could not breathe. Blanks were fired by our ears. Since all of us were tortured together, no-one talked, for fear of what the others would think. The night before, another man had been captured. We could hear his screams. Being alone, he talked under the same treatment. Had any of us been alone, we probably would have too.

After twenty minutes I was the first to be cut down and taken away to a truck. The others were told that I had spilled everything, so they needed to only conform to it. The trick did not work, and no-one talked. We were released shortly thereafter to finish the march back to the rendezvous.

I have often wondered how I would react under torture. This time I did not give in, and when I asked why I had been released first, I was told that I was the only one calm and not snivelling. This was nothing compared to what some must suffer under the Soviets and other communists.

This week marks the midpoint of training – three months since I started the course. The best is yet to come. Even now, we are better trained than most soldiers of other armies. Next week we'll be in the wilds and should see some big game. I'm glad I've come here and know that I'll be best prepared for survival. It has been exciting here, but, when things slow down, I really miss home. I think of the summer evenings, the quiet weekends, the good music, the crickets and the birds, the lake, and the coming autumn season. There is nothing here to match that. But

I can't turn back now. I have committed myself too deeply. Still, I am sure I shall be with my family again, some day.

I've been going to Baptist church services. The Gospel is preached there, but I have decided to go elsewhere because these Baptists are convinced that the Zionist takeover of Palestine is the fulfilment of Biblical prophecy. They believe that the second coming of Christ is near, and think they have the Revelation figured out completely. They expect to be 'raptured' away from the coming terror to help Christ rule in the Millennium. I remind them of Christ's words, "My kingdom is not of this world … no man knoweth the hour when the Son of God shall come again." But they choose to ignore that.

1 September 1972

I am spending four days resting and recuperating in Bulawayo after another great adventure in the Zambezi Valley. This completes fifteen weeks of basic training, and, when I return to Salisbury next Monday, the specialist courses begin, starting with demolitions.

On Thursday, 24 August, my troop left for counter-insurgency (COIN) exercises in the Nyakasanga Controlled Hunting and Rekometjie Research Station areas, north of the settlement of Makuti, and not far from Kariba. The purpose of this is to prepare us for the type of fighting taking place in Mozambique and on the border of Rhodesia: hunting down terrorist infiltrators.

Just after Makuti, the top of the Zambezi escarpment overlooks the vast, dry, desolate, but magnificent and foreboding Zambezi Valley, stretching to the northern horizon. We were now in central Africa.

Driving down the escarpment into the Valley, we were blasted with hot air like that from a furnace. The dirt road took us through thick bush, dry and barren at this time of year from lack of moisture.

All the seasonal rivers were dry, except for a few pools where antelope, bush pig, buffalo and elephant gathered. On reaching our campsite by a dry reverbed, the colour sergeant commented, "Well Coey, you are now in darkest Africa." Big trees with flat sprays of branches shaded our camp. The escarpment spread from east to west like a huge wall. I have never seen anything quite like this before. It is African and nothing else. The heat was unbearable, the misery compounded by swarms of tsetse flies and other insects.

Basecamp was set up in normal army routine: a defence perimeter with vehicles and the command group in the centre. We each dug a 'shell scrape', or shallow trench, to cover our arc of defence. Although there was little danger of attack, no chances were taken as terrorists could be anywhere in the Valley.

Life in basecamp is filthy; you live in dirt. No water can be spared for washing. It is saved for cooking only. Each night we stood guard on two-hour shifts. Under the full moon I could catch the silhouette of the mountains. I could hear jumbos (elephant) trumpeting, hyenas yipping and cackling not far away, and other bush sounds. Occasionally, two red glints would stare at me out of the darkness.

At dawn we manned the defences for half an hour. This was referred to as 'stand-to', a routine performed at both first light and dusk, since these were the most likely times of attack. The sun crept over the horizon like a giant red ball, illuminating the grey mountains. We patrolled the area around a tsetse fly control and research centre.*

On Friday night we started the sequence employed by anti-terrorist units: ambush, track-down, attack of enemy basecamp, and follow-up. Our section of fifteen men was split into two groups. The main force positioned itself along the riverbank overlooking the axis of 'enemy' advance. The other group placed itself further down to cut off the escape route. The full moon cast whiteness on the riverbed. Just after midnight the machine gun let rip, but only half the others fired, since many were sleeping. The 'enemy' fled down the riverbed.

After the second skirmish, we moved up a tributary of the river into a wooded area, much like the central hardwood region in the States. The biotype had changed with altitude. What a relief it was to feel the coolness of a breeze and shade.

Again we felt the ache of weary shoulders under our burdens, and the stabbing pain of sore feet turning and twisting on sharp-edged stones.

We camped in the woods that night, carefully conserving water which had to last for the next two days.

It wasn't long until it felt good just to sit or lie down on the ground. We quickly got used to sleeping on the ground, in spite of lumps and stones. Army life is a throw-back in many ways to pioneer days. We fight, as during the Indian wars:

* Tsetse are biting flies of the genus *Glossina*, and are the vectors of human sleeping sickness and animal trypanosomiasis. In Rhodesia they occur only in hot, low-lying areas such as the Zambezi Valley.

tracking, stalking and ambushing. We depend on our legs to get us to inaccessible areas never seen by tourist or civilian. We can live off the land if need be. This is the soldier's way of life, even at the approach of the 21st century. Yet many people consider us advanced.

Skirmishing is the typical style of fighting done by the security forces. It is hard work and not very exciting, and, as one sergeant quipped, "Not like the movies, huh, Coey?" The terrorists work in small bands and often are not seen at all, but our troops move towards the sound of their fire, shooting into places where they might be. Mortar and air support target likely spots also. When shooting begins, all take cover, throw off packs, crawl, observe, and fire. Some fire while others advance, then they change around. It is a matter of chance if you hit the enemy, or he hits you, but superior numbers and firepower win the firefight. It's a matter of who keeps whose head down, and the probability is that someone will be hit. Such is border fighting.

On Thursday, 31 August, we drove out to the Matopos National Park south of Bulawayo. It was here where, last July, I visited the grave of Cecil John Rhodes. The grave is cut into the rock on top of a large granite whale-back dwala, and, in accordance with his will, a bronze plate covers it and bears the inscription, 'Here lie the remains of Cecil John Rhodes'. The site, known as World's View, is also the final resting place of two other men of the Round Table conspiracy, Leander Star Jameson and the first prime minister of Rhodesia, Sir Charles Coghlan. One could tell that none were Christians. Nearby is a monument that contains the remains of Major Allan Wilson and his men, massacred by the Matabele in December 1893. It was a sort of 'Custer's Last Stand'.

At another spot is an inscription, 'This ground is consecrated and set apart for ever to be the resting place of those who have deserved well of their country', meaning Rhodes and the others. There are some pictures and photocopies of Rhodes's will and writings. One part reveals, in a speech made by Rhodes in mid-1899, his reference to the policy of 'equality of rights for every civilized man south of the Zambezi'. Rhodes presumed that all men who could write their place of residence, and occupation, and who worked or held property, were civilized.

Here is the resting place of a great man, but one who played an important role in the international conspiracy. He did much to expand the British Empire, but only for personal wealth. He died an atheist. The view from that hilltop is magnificent, overlooking the entire region known as the Matopos. I think it is significant and symbolic of Rhodes's life. He had such a vision for world federation, but it was material in nature only. That mountain is barren, sterile rock, overrun by blue-headed lizards.

10 September 1972

Training continues in earnest. This week was devoted to demolitions – three days of lectures, one day of practice, and exams on Friday. These courses are far more intense than any I ever had at Ohio State University.

I put on a good showing for the USA on Wednesday on a fifteen-mile endurance speed march. I finished number one on the first ten-mile segment in one hour and fifty minutes. Each of us then had to carry a man and his pack and rifle (in addition to your own) one-hundred yards. Our packs weighed about forty-eight pounds. Then we had to hike another five miles back to camp. Two others caught up with me, and we finished together in three hours and ten minutes, twenty minutes ahead of time. I always do the best I can on these tests, because Rhodesians often judge Americans by the way they perform. This time, at least, a Yank showed 'em how.

It is heartening to see how much guts some of these soldiers have. Some finished this march on raw, bloody feet. One had a broken foot, and I could read the excruciating pain written on his face.

Recently I read a news article about a terrorist landmine explosion near Mana Pools, where we actually had our counter-insurgency exercises. We in fact heard the blast.*

No-one realized at the time how near we were to a real contact.

Thursday, while on demolitions practice, we spent half the morning putting out grass fires set off by our explosives. I wanted to fight forest fires at one time, so I have now had my day at it. It is really tough work.

* The incident John is referring to occurred on 30 August 1972, when a white farmer travelling with his family in the Mana Pools Game Reserve, detonated a landmine with the right front wheel of his Citroën car. He suffered a leg amputation as a result of his injuries, but, miraculously, his wife and their three children survived relatively unscathed.

CHAPTER 10
Political Compromise and Betrayal

16 September 1972

I have been considering my own position and what I ought to do. The September *South African Observer* reports some of the agreements made between prime minister Smith and the British delegates. Among them are:

1. Unimpeded progress towards black majority rule in Rhodesia;
2. The stationing of foreign troops;
3. The ending of racial discrimination in Rhodesian schools;
4. An increase in black members of parliament so that they will eventually exceed the number of white MPs;
5. Coupling of the Rhodesian dollar to the British pound.

These agreements would destroy the European civilization of this country*. The 'Hero of '65' (Smith) has obviously succumbed to the anti-Western forces in London.

Again, it is obvious to me that there are no politicians or governments that one can fight for or trust. The fight for Western civilization is not on the battlefield, but in the realm of the intellectual, spiritual, and psychological.

As much as I would like to go on the officers' course, I may take advantage of the provisions of my contract and leave the army before I commit myself for too many years. The army is a good one and does a tremendous job of border patrol and control, but these qualities will be to no avail if the politicians sell out.

Rhodesia was lucky to escape the last settlement plans. But there is hope, since they are race-conscious, and wary of Smith. I'm still not certain what I will do.

Terrorist attacks on Rhodesia and the Portuguese territories are mounting; the entire squadron has been called out for duty. After I complete training, I'll be seeing action before the end of the year. Although military activities are strictly defensive, the army is supported and not hindered by the people and the government.

23 September 1972

Training is really going rapidly now. This week we completed courses in first aid and rock climbing. On Thursday we went to a nearby quarry and rappelled or climbed down sheer rock cliffs about seventy feet high.

I was scared to death when I first looked down, but it was really fun after I got the hang of it.

Then I couldn't do it enough. We shall be doing radio and communications during the next two weeks, and then it's back to the bush for our last endurance exercise, a week somewhere near Lake Kariba.

Some films were shown this week. One was a propaganda film produced by the Portuguese government about its anti-terrorist war in Mozambique. The Portuguese commandos, before going to battle, visit the ancient chapels erected by the first explorers and settlers in the 1500s. This reminds them that they are fighting for an ancient tradition and a prosperous future. The 'Porks', as the Portuguese are called here, must be supported, for they hold the line in their African territories for the Christian West. Another film was shown by the chaplain in an attempt to teach some of these bastards decency and morality. The film was a complete abortion because it was too long and boring, and the sound could not be heard.

Springtime and warm weather have come to Rhodesia again. The heat makes tempers short, and the bickering, arguing, and bitching that goes on sometimes becomes unbearable. Many are hardly more than schoolboys and act like little kids. This is the type desired most by the politicians, because they don't think, but just do as they are told.

SAS basic training is perhaps the best of any Western country, although I hear that the training of the South African paratroopers, the 'Parabats', is much more severe and strict. But ours is certainly better than that of the US army or Marines. Having watched news pictures of US soldiers in action, I don't wonder that there are so many casualties, the way you see them bunching up and not changing positions under fire.

As one of our training officers says, "No wonder the Yanks are losing in Vietnam."

26 September 1972

I met a new recruit who had been a corporal in the South Africa army. He is another professional soldier, tired of his inactivity there, and who has come north to fight for his people in the country of his birth. He feels that he should be in the bush, fighting the enemies of his people. He had many interesting observations on the future of southern Africa.

He claims that the Israelis are instigating much of the trouble in central Africa, and are working for the communists. Should South Africa drive north, Israel would not hesitate to attack North Africa.

His brother was a mercenary in the Congo, fighting especially the white nuns. He nearly went mad from the experience and has not yet fully recovered.

I don't know how much stock to place in his disclosures, but he seems knowledgeable. At any rate, here is a man motivated by loyalty to his civilization. It is encouraging to know that there are such as he around. I want to fight together with this type of man.

Rhodesians and South Africans are happy to see the Ugandans and Tanzanians fighting. The memory of the Mau Mau and the Simbas remains strong.

My South African friend claims that the Zulus and related peoples in southern Africa hate the Africans to the north. Should these more centrally-located tribes attack south of the Zambezi, the Zulus would fight against them.

During the Anglo-Boer War of 1899–1902, it was the Boers who introduced the style of guerrilla warfare now so common in modern conflicts. They first used sniping, ambush, hit-and-run, and bush warfare against the British, who cried 'unfair'. The South Africans are a fighting people, and the West needs them badly.

27 September 1972

There is a difference between soldiers of the SAS and other paratroopers. The former are infiltrators, and parachuting is only one means of getting behind enemy lines. Other means include scuba diving, canoeing, driving Land Rovers, or simply going by foot. On the other hand, the typical paratroopers are just airborne infantry, trained to jump into battle.

29 September 1972

One sergeant yesterday observed that most civilians do not recognize the danger of communism because they think it does not directly affect them in their daily lives. Although most younger people are not particularly disloyal to their country, they certainly lack fervent national feeling.

A South African told me how many in his country feel secure because South West Africa and Mozambique provide buffers from attack. The ignorance may be fatal to them.

CHAPTER 11
'All In'

30 September 1972

My best friend, George Jenkinson, is the perfect gentleman, showing the best genotypic characteristics of his Scottish and aristocratic French ancestry. He is the prototype of chivalry: brave, gentle, thoroughly Christian, and never speaks a foul word. He stays cool and calm. Even under the harshest harassment. He is an outstanding athlete with tremendous physical endurance, but prefers the soft life of the university he had left. His kind-heartedness allows lesser men to take advantage of him at times.

14 October 1972

I think the Christian soldier should be, as was said of the Confederate general, Robert E. Lee, 'a foe without hate, a friend without treachery, a soldier without cruelty … a public officer without vice, a private citizen without wrong, a Christian without hypocrisy. He ought to strive to be Caesar without his ambition, Frederick without his tyranny, and Napoleon without his selfishness'.

15 October 1972

Tomorrow the big training exercise commences, called 'All In'. The purpose of it is to test the skills learned over previous weeks in one big commando operation at Inyanga. The training troop will be divided into two six-man teams, one to reconnoitre the police station, the other to make its way from the Inyangombe Falls to World's View to meet agents who are coming to instruct us in the missions we are to accomplish – blowing up designated targets. This is the type of infiltration mission we would do during wartime.

16-21 October 1972

On Monday evening the training troop left on its mission by rail from Msasa East station, just outside Salisbury. We travelled in a boxcar, and it reminded me of Lenin and his army of criminals when they secretly crossed Germany by rail for the 1917 revolution. About 0100 hours we were let off at some rail siding and taken by truck to the drop-off point somewhere around Mount Domba, a few miles from the village of Juliasdale. This put us once again in the Eastern Highlands.

This exercise is what I consider to be a true commando operation. My squad made a giant sweep from west to south into the Inyangombe River valley, covering the rugged savannah country. We travelled night and day, taking only a few breaks to catch an hour or two of sleep. The first rendezvous was a small hydro-power station on the Inyangombe River. It took us two days to get there, since we used an indirect route through the thickest bush to make our *spoor* (trail) difficult to follow.

At one point we dived for cover when a para-transporter* suddenly flew over. We were right in the middle of the 'enemy' drop zone, so hastened to get away fast. Fortunately no-one found our tracks, but the other patrol was ambushed and three members captured, so eliminating its effectiveness. My patrol was then assigned its tasks: to reconnoitre the bridge over the Inyangombe and the police station, to set up charges, and to disrupt the 'enemy' lines of communication.

We made the power station that Wednesday night having crossed the deep, swift and treacherous Inyangombe River. From there we were told to carry on towards the village and set charges on the bridge. On the way we nearly stumbled onto the 'enemy' patrol, but they did not see us. Later we crept past the police station in stocking feet while the 'enemy' slept, and placed charges on their vehicles. Obviously since this was only a training exercise, so no explosives were detonated.

The rest of Thursday, in the sweltering heat, we climbed up the mountain to World's View, where we had the most spectacular view of the highlands I have ever seen. There are extremes of weather on the mountains, blistering sun by day, and cold and windy in nights that bring surprising rains. Another 'agent' met us at the top, and told us to proceed to a small lake at Troutbeck to recover some explosives for the final demolition job. By letting ourselves down by ropes, we hid for several hours on the face of the cliff so we could rest and not be seen. We would have been noticed on the open plateau above.

Friday afternoon we crossed the open ground and hid in a pine wood by the lake until dark. Four of us, using snorkels and fins, swam across the lake to the dam wall, packed the explosives, and then swam back. The lost members of the patrol joined us, and we all set off for the pine forests and the high ground. Several

* Douglas C-47 / DC-3 Skytrain, known in Rhodesia by the Royal Air Force designation, Dakota.

miles away we set charges in a small abandoned hut and blew it up early Saturday morning. Mission ended.

I really had the time of my life this week, and I could enjoy it. The exercise was more difficult than the other two, but it wasn't as hard on us physically because we were fit for it. There is an early period when I feel exhausted, but then I adjust to the strain and can carry on indefinitely, despite lack of sleep and little to eat. There is something about the mountains that is invigorating and keeps me going; otherwise, I might drop from exhaustion.

It is apparent how much planning and preparation must go into a raid to make it successful.

One can avoid leaving trails by travelling at night, walking over rocks instaed of leaving tracks on soft ground, and moving upstream several yards during a crossing. The training is excellent, but there is so much more to know, and we get only the basics. The six months is nearly up now. Three more weeks of paratrooping and I'll be through. It has been a hard grind, but well worth it.

23 October 1972

I spoke with a corporal who told me that he always tries to look into the future as best he can. He figures that the outlook is not good, and so he strives to get the most from each moment, indulging a great deal in sex and immediate pleasures. He always tries to give the impression of being a sex fiend, but deep inside he is searching for the meaning of life. He is always good to new recruits and wants to help them become men. Whether he rejects God or not is hard to say. Once he told us that, if there really is a God, why doesn't He come down and show Himself when challenged to fight. But this may just have been a pose.

The troops have left again for more action in Kariba, and most of the RLI has been sent over into Mozambique.* The rest of us will join the squadron as soon as we complete the para-course.

Today the course was debriefed on its 'All In' exercise. Only five passed, including me and George Jenkinson. This means that there are only five still left on the course, out of the thirty-seven men who began the original two courses. Several have been permitted to carry on with the para-course, but have to do another 'All

* Operation Sable, the RLI's first battalion-size operation into Mozambique, a follow-on from SAS operations in the area.

In' exercise at Kariba.

The para-course begins today. It is run by the air force, since the Rhodesian army does not have a jump school of its own.

There is a simple song sung by the troops. Somehow I find it appealing. It's called *Butterfly*:

Butterfly, my butterfly,
I'll come home to you one day,
Butterfly, my butterfly,
Wait for me. Don't fly away.

CHAPTER 12
Paratroop Training

There are some jokes going around about paratrooping. When fitting a helmet, get one a bit large, because the head swells after the first jump.

27 October 1972

The para-course is taught at the main air force base, New Sarum, just outside Salisbury. The instructors are superb – two short Irishmen, a Briton who used to be in the British SAS, and some other Rhodesians, all dedicated to teaching their skill. Old American Douglas C-47 twin-propeller aircraft are used for para-transport, but the latest US-made parachutes are available.

The first week is spent in group training in preparation for exit, descent, and landing. All actions seem strange and peculiar, for jumping is really an unnatural act for humans. It can be mastered only by strict self-discipline and by learning new mechanical routines. We fall and roll on mats, and jump from platforms to learn the routine and drill that gets you safely from the aircraft to the ground a thousand feet below. We will do eight jumps, starting on 31 October.

I met an American chap, newly arrived in Rhodesia, who had been a paratrooper in the 82nd Airborne Division in Vietnam. He is interested in joining the Rhodesian army, and I attempted to sell him on the SAS. He came here for much the same reasons I did: the deterioration of the US army, and the infiltration of so many communists and communist sympathizers into the State Department. He says that his unit was full of heroin addicts when he left.

The other American in the SAS has deserted and gone back to San Diego. He came here seeking action, but didn't find it.

29 October 1972

I am still unsure of where I should make my stand for my beliefs and my civilization. Should I stay in Rhodesia, or should I return to my fatherland to do what I can for America, our principal bulwark of freedom?

I want to be a soldier, a warrior, a Crusader for my God and country, and to fight the hell-inspired enemy that would crush every delicate and beautiful creation of this world. I want to be a free man, the master of my own destiny, not a pawn of usurpers and traitors who manipulate the masses into subservience. I want to do God's will and fulfil the purpose of my creation. I want this, but I just don't know how to go about it.

I am willing and eager to do my part of the bush fighting and to guard the borders, but peace won't come until the war is taken to the enemy, and he learns the fighting superiority of the European, the Western man, over the barbarian.

But the greater battle is for Western people to regain control of their nations and destinies, and to drive out the usurpers, aliens, and traitors that run our governments. May Christ and the warrior Archangel Michael inspire us.

3 November 1972

Today we did our first real parachuting, and it is an exhilarating experience. We've done four jumps this week, and we'll do four more next week. We get up at four in the morning for early-morning flights when the wind is calmer, and we report to the airfield for parachute fittings and a final debrief. As the flight sergeant inspects us, we lean over while he gives a mighty tug on the webbing, squeezing out our breath and leaving us in a hunched position. We secure our helmets and march out to the Dakota.

As the plane warms up, taxis down the runway, and lifts off, there is a mix of behaviour on board. Some joke and laugh merrily, one thumbs nonchalantly through a magazine, one whistles while fidgeting with his reserve 'chute, some doze, and some just sit in silence, ashen-faced, wondering why they are there.

Finally, your own turn comes to jump, and the flight sergeant bellows the following sequence:

"Prepare for action." You stand up and hook onto the static line and check equipment.

"Tell off for equipment check."

The last man of the stick* shouts, "Five, okay," and then down to the first, "Okay, stick, okay."

"Action stations." The stick clomps down to the hatch and stops.

* A stick was the army term used for a patrol unit of four men. This was an effective number for operating in the bush, as well as the number that could be rapidly deployed in an Alouette III helicopter. One of the members of a stick would usually carry a light machine gun, the MAG.

"Stand at the door." The first man prepares to jump.

"Go … and go … and go …" The stick leaps out.

You stand in the door with the roar of the engines and the wind in your ears. You are scared, but you concentrate so much on the jumping sequence and procedure that there is no time to think or hesitate. You leap into space. The wind catches and hurls you back and down. There is a sudden tug as the 'chute opens, and suddenly all is quiet. You sweep swiftly through the clear, cool, morning silence in your own little mushroom. There is no sensation of falling. The feeling of freedom and flying is the greatest.

You look up at the canopy, kick out the seat strap, put your legs and feet together, reach up for the suspension straps, and look down. The earth rushes up at you as you drift along. It gets closer and closer, your feet touch, and – *ka-wap* – over you tumble. You are home. The landing is hard, but the shock is dissipated by the roll.

Watching the others come down, you notice all eyes peering over the reserve 'chute and under the rim of the tin helmet as they land.

The whole drop takes only forty-five to sixty seconds. Once you land, you have an overwhelming feeling of satisfaction, pride … and relief. You are now a paratrooper. It is good to overcome your fears and to gain confidence after more jumps. You even enjoy it after a while.

You roll up your canopy, pack everything away, and walk back to the truck. Everyone is full of tales to tell. There are complaints of sore heels, legs, heads, and butts.

I had hard landings on the first two jumps, which made me a bit hesitant on the third.

The night before I was so anxious that I could hardly sleep, and I had nightmares of breaking bones. But my fears were unwarranted. The third was the best yet, and the landing gentle.

Others have joined us on this para-course, coming from all parts of the Commonwealth. One officer had served in Vietnam with the New Zealand SAS, and another had been in Northern Ireland with the British 1st Battalion Parachute Regiment (1 Para). A couple of the instructors had served in Egypt with the British army in the 1950s. It is all quite an assortment.

There is one more week of jumping left, and we will have completed basic and specialist training. The five of us left will then be posted as troopers into the squadron. The ceremony will be delayed until 15 December when another group will also be passing-out (graduating).

In the meantime, we will go with the squadron for action somewhere in Mozambique, sometimes still referred to as Portuguese East Africa. It is significant, I think, that the Portuguese territories are often simply called 'Portugal'. They are considered part of that European country, and fly its flag. The inhabitants, black and white, are citizens.

Although the greatest danger to southern Africa is from the conspiracy's workings in governmental and economic spheres, it is still necessary at present to fight the terrorist aggression with military operations. I am willing to fight for Rhodesia and Portugal, for the time being anyhow, because both are worth fighting for. Neither has descended yet to the position of the United States, although they are headed that way.

I have been taught that one should be soldier, warrior, and Crusader for God, country, or anything worth fighting for. I was born a thousand years too late for the Crusades, and few are now willing to make the world safe for Christianity. It seems that under present conditions one cannot be a soldier without furthering the aims of the internationalists, the liberals, the Council on Foreign Relations (CFR), the Zionists, or other alien groups. But I believe it is a Christian's duty to oppose the enemies of his civilization, just as much as it is to save souls. I have heard it said that freedom is God-given, and only given to those who are willing to fight for it, even if it means opposing the state.

Shortly before I left the States, my brother told me that once one understands the cause of trouble in our civilization, the conspiracy to rule the world, then it becomes imperative for that person to oppose it. All else becomes irrelevant and superficial. The struggle is more than dabbling in politics, for it concerns the survival of civilization as we know it. Our defeat means that the world will be thrust into a dark age of terror and slavery.

4 November 1972

I suspect that because of Nixon's precise timing for possibly terminating US involvement in Vietnam, he will be re-elected. The people want the damn thing ended, no matter how dishonourable the withdrawal or how severe the consequences. Some observers believe it is only to free us for action in the Middle East.

At Ticonderoga, Bunker Hill, Brandywine, the Alamo, Gettysburg, San Juan Hill, Guadalcanal and countless other battles, the American has proven that he will, on the battlefield, defeat any enemy that threatens his freedom. The modern American must reckon with an enemy outside the gate, who looks, acts, and speaks the same, but who uses warfare of another dimension. This new enemy uses weapons more dangerous than bullets or missiles. He can stop the flow of culture and traditions between generations.

Is the American Republic dead? Will it go the way of Rome? Will Richard Nixon be the Augustus who terminates American liberty? Soon we will know.

If we are worthy of our ancestors who gave us liberty, and if we are to bequeath freedom to the next generation, we must, as Burns wrote:

> 'Lay the proud usurper low …
> Welcome to your gory bed,
> Or to victory …'

11 November 1972

Yesterday I completed the para-course and basic training. We did another four jumps, and that qualifies us as paratroopers. I still get nervous in the plane, but it is a relief to get out of the cramped fuselage and into the open sky. The last jump was open to spectators, and several families came to watch our mass drop. Two blokes collided in the air, and the rope holding the equipment pack of one got looped around the neck of the other, almost strangling him. This incident provided a lot of excitement. After landing, we lined up, and the air force officer commanding the para-school gave one of the weakest speeches I have ever heard. All he could say was, "Well done," in not so concise a manner. Next month, however, we will have more of a ceremony. So I have earned my wings and fawn-coloured beret, and know now that I could have made Special Forces had I gone into the US army.

CHAPTER 13
22nd Birthday and Passing-Out

13 November 1972

Yesterday was my twenty-second birthday. Upon reflection, I believe that my twenty-first was uneventful, but full of purpose and significance. I began to live for my beliefs and actively oppose the enemies of my country. I graduated from Ohio State University, became an expatriate by immigrating to Rhodesia, and proved myself with the SAS.

I left today for my first active tour of duty in the bush, a border-control operation based at Gutsa, in the Centenary district in the Zambezi Valley. I am back again to the heat of central Africa, positioned just below the escarpment. The camp is fortified with earthen walls and bunkers, and is provided with washing facilities and open-sided bunkhouses for sleeping.

14 November 1972

Four troopers and I left the permanent basecamp of Gutsa for a patrol to the Hunyani Mission to the north-west, in the neighbouring Dande TTL in Sipolilo district, and just a few hundred yards from the Mozambique border. The mission is run by an American Baptist, so it seems ironic that, after coming all the way over here, my first assignment is to guard one of my countrymen.

Although we are just lying around in the shade today, we start patrolling again tomorrow. When our commander briefed us on the situation last night, he commented that the missionary here is "inquisitive, but on our side" ... supposedly. I just hate to think what might happen to him if the terrorists come after we leave.

There are eight of us at the mission, constituting two four-man patrols. Each goes out on alternate mornings, dropped off by truck along a dirt track running parallel to the border.

Some terrs* have deserted to the Portuguese side where they are employed to guard the fenced-in farms in remote areas. They wear black uniforms and are referred to as militia. Sometimes they cause confusion as they still carry communist-made weapons.

* Most in the country, civilian and military, referred to the insurgents as terrs. The regular infantry units later started using the Korean War slang word, gook.

The anti-terrorist campaign is psychological in some aspects, in that it is a contest of winning the support of the rural Africans, who prefer white soldiers as they leave their women alone. The army goes out of its way to keep friendly relations, and to respect and protect African property. For instance, while driving out to the mission, we hit a chicken on the road. The owner claimed that it was his prize chicken, so we paid him a dollar for it, which was much more than what it was worth. The Africans respond by reporting strangers and suspected terrorists in the area.

17 November 1972

I was on patrol again today. As expected, we saw and found nothing. The heat is terrific now, making everyone irritable.

A band of militia from Mozambique, led by a Portuguese officer, arrived at a village just over the border from us, where we met him at the mission store. Since we couldn't communicate, both parties just stood and eyed each other uneasily. After going through two interpreters, from English to the local dialect to Portuguese, we invited the officer to our camp for dinner. He is a mean, hard-looking fellow, who has a throwing knife strapped to his shoulder which, no doubt, he knew how to use. He gives me the impression of being intelligent and knowing. Unfortunately, our communication bogged down in the really awkward translation. His patrol had made contact with a terr earlier, but both sides pushed off after exchanging a few rounds – the usual reaction. His patrol took on fresh provisions at the store and returned to its basecamp.

Whenever armed men, whether Porks or terrs arrive in Mozambique, the villages on our side of the border become flooded with refugees.

26 November 1972

Since becoming a trooper, I have mixed more with the other squadron members. It is evident that I can never really become a part of them, not on a social basis anyhow. Their ways and mine are too different. Most are good blokes, and I respect them, but they mostly live for pleasure, drinking and whoring. The Christian soldier is sometimes despised and ridiculed.

27 November 1972

About half the squadron was put on standby for an operation in Mozambique.

I volunteered to go, but I was refused as the more senior, and therefore more experienced, members go in first. The commander said that my para-wings still smell of the quartermaster store, and that I would have to sit this one out.

I received a letter from Mr Brown saying he would print a second letter of mine, but he is leery about printing my real name. He warned me that I am 'not allowed to take part in politics'. I told him to use my real name anyhow, and that, if the Smith government could not stand the criticism, then I am prepared for the consequences. I just believe that proper identification of authority is something that goes along with the freedom of press and speech.

I loaned my US army training manuals to my old training sergeant at Gwelo. When one considers how uptight this army gets about any of its printed material, I think it is amusing that the School of Infantry was gleaning all the information they could from my manuals.

1 December 1972

I did my ninth jump this morning, for exhibition before a new intake of recruits. No matter how many jumps one does, the feeling of nervousness, butterflies, and downright fright, always seem to occur once on the plane.

I attended the premier of an SAS recruiting flick [film] that will do much for an improved public opinion of us. The squadron needs an heroic public image, and legends must be created about it.

2 December 1972

I received a Christmas card from home, which is very meaningful. A verse is added which says: 'Ultimately the Nativity is all the hope we have'.

7 December 1972

Last Monday I left for another 'All In' exercise, this time in an area which includes Penhalonga and Lake Alexander, near the eastern-border town of Umtali. This time I did the chasing instead of being chased.

The whole squadron was mass-dropped early Tuesday morning onto a beautifully soft ploughed field. This was my tenth, and perhaps last jump if I leave the army next year. We are in the Eastern Highlands again. It is bushy and green from abundant rains. Some parts are intensely forested with commercial plantations of eucalyptus. The area around the little village of Penhalonga, with its mining, forests, and sawmills, remind me of the Hocking Hills of Ohio. The savannah, however, is predominant.

Tracking groups set off, and, anticipating the route of the 'insurgent force', ambush and stop groups took up positions on Tuesday night and Wednesday. My group, unfortunately, was in the wrong place, and we saw nothing the whole time. We slept and went hungry.

Wednesday afternoon we pulled out and stayed the night at a caravan park in Penhalonga. The town held a candlelight service right next to us, at which the townsfolk were happy to have us join them in the singing of Christmas carols. I enjoy nothing more than attending religious services with fellow soldiers. On rare occasions such as this, some of them show signs of faith.

The squadron was mentioned in *Newsweek* magazine of 27 November, in a report on our recent border-control operations to keep the route to Beira in Mozambique open. The article referred to us as, 'Rhodesia's crack Special Air Service', and we all got a big charge out of that.

15 December 1972

Our passing-out parade was held today at the New Sarum air force base, at which those of us who completed training this year were formally presented with our [para] wings. The whole squadron marched past the reviewing dais of army brass to the stirring marches of the RAR band playing, *Lili Marlene*, *March of the Belgian Paratroopers*, and Wagner's *Flight of the Valkyries.* A tremendous swelling pride overwhelmed me when these were played, and I couldn't help but grin. This was our brief moment of glory.

Course 4/72 marched proudly forward to receive their wings. Ours is the first course in a new phase of a hardening of discipline and acceptance standards for the SAS. The squadron proudly marched a pass-in-review with precision drill in front of the lovely ladies in their floppy, broad-brimmed hats, and colourful dresses.

The squadron's new honorary colonel delivered a short address on the history of the SAS, and the background of the wings design, which was taken from an ancient Egyptian hieroglyph, with the parachute replacing the bird.

The parade today meant far more to me that even my graduation from Ohio State University. I have proven myself worthy of this unit, and in my mind I know

I could have made Special Forces in the States. Despite all the training, however, I have the feeling that there is much more still to do and to learn.

My best friend, George Jenkinson, won the 'Recruit of the Course' and the 'Recruit of the Year' awards. He really deserves them. I was in the running for a while, but the sergeant major and I had different ideas, and didn't see eye-to-eye in some things. Too often I was shot down for doing things my own way.

Four of us, including George and I, have been chosen to go before the Officer Selection Board.

CHAPTER 14
Christmas in South Africa

20 December 1972

This morning I crossed the South Africa border, at once noticing a distinct transition. Because of irrigation, the land was suddenly green again. I stayed for a while in a small Afrikaans-speaking town* where once the British were holed up under siege for several months during the Anglo-Boer War of 1899–1902.

My immediate impression of this country is that is much more nationalistic than Rhodesia. One feels that he is in a nation, comparable to being in America, rather than being in a colony or area of colonial status.

The music on the radio is pleasant to listen to – no hard rock. There is a station for English and one for Afrikaans.

Before I left, I learned of a new wave of terrorist attacks across the border into Rhodesia, both from Mozambique and an occasional foray from Botswana. All the forces were called out, but George and I were not recalled from leave. Some farms were machine-gunned, and soldiers have been injured by landmines, but no-one has been killed yet, except for some of the terrorists†

21 December 1972

Johannesburg is a large metropolitan area, the biggest in southern Africa – perhaps the largest in Africa, for that matter. I was happy to quickly leave there for Pretoria, only forty miles away.

Pretoria is a capital of South Africa. The seat of the South African administration, it is a beautiful place, with many Dutch-style and colonial-type houses, with immaculately cultivated and maintained gardens. Most of the people here are Afrikaners of Dutch extraction, and I find them impressive. Despite their earthy mien, they are cultured, attending Shakespearian plays and classical concerts. They

* In his journal, John gives the name of this town as Mphoengs, but this tiny settlement is on the border between Zimbabwe and Botswana. It never has been Afrikaans-speaking. Mafeking (now Mahikeng) lies in South Africa near its border with Botswana, and was the only town in the region under siege during the Anglo-Boer War.

† During the night of 21 December, a gang of nine ZANLA terrorists attacked the homestead on Altena Farm in the Centenary district, north of Salisbury. Two nights later, the neighbouring Whistlefield Farm was also attacked. Terrorists planted landmines in the immediate area. These landmark attacks heralded the commencement of a new and much-intensified phase of the insurgents' war against Rhodesia.

are a conservative people, but must have a strong leader to follow, like Dr Hendrik Verwoerd was.

There are still some difficulties and hard feelings between the Afrikaners and English whites that have carried over from the Anglo-Boer War, the main point of friction being that the English are liberal. After the war, the Afrikaners were often regarded as second-class citizens until the 1920s. Not until the 1950s did they come to dominate South African politics.

29 December 1972

On 21 December I met with S.E.D. Brown, editor of the *South African Observer*, at his home,

which is located on a hillside in a Pretoria suburb. I had intended to stay only for the afternoon, but his family asked me to stay the night, and later, to stay over Christmas. The Browns made me feel so much at home. We all seemed to get on so well, that I ended up staying five days. Mr Brown must be approaching sixty, but he has a young wife and two children, aged eight and ten. By the first evening they were calling me 'Uncle John'.

Mr Brown is of both English and Afrikaans lineage, but has acquired completely British characteristics. He is a scholar, an intellectual, and a philosopher. He provides much of the leadership and guidance for the true conservatives in South Africa. His understanding of politics and insight into the conspiratorial forces are truly outstanding. He is a born aristocrat, and I think that, if he had chosen another vocation, he might have had a fortune by now. But he has completely dedicated himself to publishing the *South African Observer.*

Mr Brown is not optimistic about the fate of the West. He is convinced that Nixon, Heath, Vorster and Smith, although they pose as conservatives, are complete phonies. Each is little more than a puppet of the internationalist conspiracy. The enemy of the European in Africa is not the African, but the internationalist's and their liberal colleagues who undermine Western culture and political forms. The greatest hope is that the manipulators of the conspiracy will make a mistake – a big mistake – such as they appear to be doing in the Middle East.

People will only be aroused when their survival is threatened. Once the people recognize the instigator of troubles, no amount of propaganda in the press or education, or outright repression, can stop their vengeance.

Brown has a very dry and subtle sense of humour that at times makes you almost want to cry. His jokes always have a point.

I met several conservatives who look to Brown for guidance. He heads no organization, but people seem to revolve around his place. There are hard-core Afrikaner nationalists, fearless in standing up for their traditions and their country. There is a German woman raising her children in the Prussian tradition and custom, who had immigrated after the war. I met a Belgian doctor, formerly active in his African country, who is now organizing resistance in South Africa to the conspiracy. He has asked me to speak to one of his groups the next time I come down, and I intend to do so at the first chance I get.

Mr Brown was going to print my letter in the December issue of his paper, but at the last moment he decided not to do so. He again advised me not to reveal my name or military unit because, as he said, "There is no need to expose yourself needlessly, particularly when you may be valuable later." My letter will now appear in the January issue. The first line will be omitted, and the letter will be under the Afrikaans name, 'Johan Coetzee'.

On 26 December I flew back to Bulawayo by jet. From there George, two other chaps, and I, drove up to Victoria Falls for a couple of days. This is one of the most awe-inspiring spectacles in the world. The Zambezi River thunders over a giant cleft in the earth, caused by a fault that split hundreds of thousands of years ago. The nearby town of the same name thrives on the tourist trade. We took a ferry up the river above the falls, from where we gazed into Zambia on the opposite bank. As one European tourist commented, it is like looking over the frontier from Europe into Russia. On occasion I could see trucks taking food and other supplies over the bridge to the Zambians. This programme is sponsored by the Rhodesian government, "Criminal …," as Brown said.

I am spending the last few days of leave with the Jenkinsons. Sunday, 31 December, we return to Salisbury, where we shall prepare to leave for the officers' selection course.

Thank you for sending me the book *Captains and the Kings.* I have particularly enjoyed reading it. Taylor Caldwell has done a terrific job of exposing the CFR and how it works.

Sometimes it seems to me that I have spent a lifetime here, rather than just ten months. The New Year appears promising. Christian conservatives over here despair of waiting and hoping, but they realize that it is only a matter of time until the pendulum swings our way.

I have learned that one of our soldiers died of wounds from a landmine explosion. He was the brother of one of the instructors at the para-school.

30 December 1972

Today I attended the musical *Camelot*, and was much impressed that a current production would stress such ideals as chivalry, civilization, fairness, and 'might for right'. The story may be a myth, but the legend of King Arthur is part of our Western heritage.

CHAPTER 15
Various Viewpoints

Some of my Baptist friends proclaim that they "are in the world, but not of this world." On this basis, so many of them refuse to come to grips with the problems of our civilization. They content themselves instead waiting for Christ to come again to save them. I believe, however, that man makes his own world; some change it for the better, or at least try. For the world is of man. Evil too often rules by default – lack of opposition.

3 January 1973

I quote the Portuguese government's view of its trouble in Africa:

> To the indiscriminate massacre of those early days, we reply with the conviction of our arms. To the calumny of our enemies, we offer the honesty and the genuine and deep spirit of our nation. Our flag flew in the golden age of our great world discoveries. The Cross of Christ was raised by our forefathers on the highest hills and over the widest and most distant lands. We gave the world the full knowledge of our whole civilization. Alone, and in silence, we continue in the steps we have undertaken.
>
> To win or lose a war? May God, great, just, and mighty, decide the fate of nations, of people, or of battle. We will always have won because we will have given the best we had and the best we could offer. We extended a friendly and kindly hand to the poor, to the abandoned, teaching them the life of progress and that of the future. Before the world clamours of many nations, we remain faithful to our principles, and defend our sovereignty with the courage of our soldiers.

Here is the spirit of the Christian West, long lost in so many Western nations. If only such a feeling could be revived in Rhodesia, England, and America, our resurgence would be assured. Many look down on the Portuguese as a lesser breed, but they have given us an example. Can we do less than they?

[Censored]

What is an aristocracy? Some may say that it is the ruling class, or body, or organization. I think, perhaps, it is not so much the governor of states and nations, but the governor of ideas.

This might be a king, prime minister, or president, but certainly it is also the professor, school teacher, poet, journalist, or one in communications. It is ideas, or the lack of them, that rules nations, and whoever influences or controls these ideas, rules the nation in direct proportion.

4 January 1973

This morning I completed my eleventh parachute jump – perhaps my last. I thank God that I have completed these without injury. After several jumps, one starts thinking of all the things that could happen, making one not so eager to jump. But I still would always volunteer.

Four SAS troopers are going on the officers' selection course, including myself. Many doubt that I will make it, with some saying so openly. I think that God has led me through my hardships for a larger purpose than just to be an SAS trooper. If it is God's will for me to be an officer and to stay in this country then, by His grace, I shall once more have success. I will do my best as a representative, not only for the SAS, but also for the United States of America. I must help succeed for the glory of God, country, and family. May God help me in this endeavour.

6 January 1973

Some of the African nationalist leaders claim to be Christian, though following the Marxists. This claim emphasizes the racial and cultural conflict between European and African. The latter have turned to the communists for aid, and, thus, are used by them. It must not be forgotten that most Africans south of the Zambezi will support the white government. The African opponents of this army are volunteers, and hate their black brethren to the north.

I have no doubt that white rule of Africa is justified, because both African and European cultures can flourish and prosper under it. Some whites say this is immoral, but I think that the greatest sin and tragedy would be for the European to withdraw.

13 January 1973

Today I successfully completed phase one of the officers' selection course at the School of Infantry in Gwelo. About eighty civilians and regular soldiers converged here from all over Rhodesia in an attempt to qualify for the training programme that starts next month. Some days were given to a series of intelligence and aptitude test, and we had to write essays and give lectures. On others we were given tasks to perform on an obstacle course, such as getting men over electrified fences, over walls, and across broken bridges in a given time, all with the help of ropes, poles, and planks. This tested the leadership potential and problem-solving ability of each candidate, as judged by a board of officers ranking from lieutenants to brigadiers.

Today each of us appeared before the board to hear its evaluation. Only half were selected to continue onto phase two, which runs for the next two weeks. George, another SAS trooper, and I made it through, but our fourth member was rejected. Next weekend we go on a three-day forty-mile endurance march. But more academic work is required also, such as holding a debate and giving a short lecture, the latter with only ten minutes to prepare.

The terrorist troubles may now be escalating into more open warfare. This week the Rhodesian government closed the border posts with Zambia, cutting off the routes of that country's vitally important copper exports. Zambia must now export through Tanzania.

The landmining continues and the death toll rises. Two South African policemen* were killed; two government officials murdered and another missing. So this January offensive is quite serious.

22 January 1973

Upon returning to Gwelo, I heard that an SAS sergeant was killed in a parachute jump.†

It seems that the army intelligence service is very efficient. It knows everything that African forces to the north do and plan.

* From 1967, South Africa had deployed units from its police force into Rhodesia's north-west, ostensibly to counter the movement of South African insurgents through Rhodesia.

† Acting Sergeant Frank Wilmot was killed during a night drop into Mozambique in Rhodesia's first airborne operation since 'C' Squadron SAS had operated in Malaya. Both his main and reserve parachutes had failed to open. The target was the Muzengezi River in Mozambique, trying to track down the abducted Rhodesian Gerald Hawksworth.

The current insurgent invasion is much worse than news sources report to the public. Present conditions are similar to those of the Matabele Rebellion of 1896, including the onset of severe drought and an upsurge in the activities of tribal spirit mediums.

26 January 1973

Today God granted success again. I passed the officer selection board and will commence officer training next week. Of the original eighty, only eighteen have been chosen. George Jenkinson and another SAS man were also selected, as well as the son of South Africa's minister of defence. Another American from South Dakota was selected, but I have only spoken to him a few times. He and his family have been in Rhodesia for about two and a half years.

When I appeared before the board of officers, they gave me a good report, but told me that I take life too seriously. They said that I must project my personality and withdraw from my shell. By the grace of God, the training I receive will be used to defend the religion and civilization of my people.

CHAPTER 16
Officers' Training

3 March 1973

A people or nation must have faith in the Divine sanction of its own existence. That faith will beget freedom, but loss of that faith is the worst betrayal of our loved ones, our forebears, and our posterity.

5 March 1973

Leon Trotsky once warned that anybody who wanted to lead a peaceful life has picked the wrong century in which to be born.

April 1973

This is Holy Week, but it hasn't been observed as I would like. I still think of its significance: the fulfilment of Christ's mission on earth, his suffering and death to atone for all men's sins, and His triumph over hell and death. Christ's birth, death, and resurrection are the most important events of history.

30 April 1973

My father writes that he believes I have found my mission in life. Although I am following my destiny, I cannot yet state what my life mission is. Sometimes I wonder if I even have one, beyond what small part I play in human or national history.

It seems that nearly all the Christians and missionaries I have met in Rhodesia believe that their sole purpose is to witness for Christ. I have no objection to this whatsoever, but these people do nothing to expose the evil forces of our time, such as communism or Socialist-Zionism. They are not, in fact, convinced that these are evil, and even support the latter. If this continues, they themselves are bound to fall victim to those evils. How many devout Christians, in spite of their prayers for deliverance, have fallen victim to communism in Europe, Asia, and Africa.

26 May 1973

On Monday I attended a lecture by an army major on *The Classical War Threat to*

Rhodesia. Classical or limited war is defined as war between two or more countries, short of total world war, with the probable use of tactical nuclear weapons, or a war in a non-nuclear environment.

Classical war is the 'foundation' of all wars, for it may escalate to nuclear war. According to the theories of Mao Tse Tung, even revolutionary wars are intended to escalate to classical wars when the manpower and materials are available. 'The ultimate threat of revolutionary wars is classical war'.

In Rhodesia, according to the major, the threat of classical war comes from three sources, all of which are enemies of white southern Africa:

1. The internal threat of blacks seeking independence in isolated countries, eg Zimbabwe and Namibia. There is no strategic ambition in this. Territorial ambition is limited to individual status, but there is economic ambition. The threat of internal subversion with external support could escalate into a conventional war if the communist powers intervene after an African setback.

2. Another threat is communist domination of the world. The communists have territorial and economic ambitions in Africa. South Africa produces enormous quantities of gold a year. If South Africa were taken, the Soviets would dominate a gold-backed economy, while the West attempts to free itself from the gold standard.

Rhodesia has a wealth of minerals. There is also strategic ambition, for the ports in South Africa are the best on the continent. Control of the Cape would give the Soviets domination of the Indian and South Atlantic oceans, a considerable advantage in a confrontation with NATO. Control by the communist bloc would double the cost of shipping oil. The West would be forced to use the long route from the Middle East, over the Indian and Pacific Oceans, instead of the shorter route around the Cape to the Atlantic Ocean.

For this reason, the Soviets are recognized as enemies. This is why the Western powers should oppose a Soviet attack on South Africa. The communists say, however, that an attack is unlikely, for time is on their side. They will eventually take over without a war.

3. The third threat is the support of African 'liberation' movements by the

> United Nations. The UN passively supports African states with economic and political aid, but as a body it has no economical or territorial ambitions. Presently, it is a cold-war confrontation, but the UN could intervene militarily. The Rhodesian army recognizes that a UN peacekeeping force would be composed of only African countries, perhaps because the major powers would not want to participate.

I know they are wrong in this analysis because they fail to recognize the power of the internationalists who researched an invasion of South Africa, but found it too difficult at the time. (This was the battle plan drawn up by the Carnegie Endowment for World Peace).

The major continued:

> There is the Sino-Soviet clash to consider also. It seems that the African Marxists can identify themselves more easily with the 'coloured' yellow men of China than the Russians, who are white. There are 15,000 Chinese military personnel in Tanzania, far outnumbering the entire Tanzanian army. The Chinese have greater influence south of the Equator, the Russians north of it.
>
> The objectives in southern Africa are the gold and ports of South Africa. The key to southern Africa is Rhodesia. Angola and Mozambique are not of great value for the ultimate objective, because South Africa is not so vulnerable to aggression from them. They could only give material and economic support for wars of 'liberation'.
>
> Rhodesia, however, if it fell, would provide good communications with the north, especially Zambia and Tanzania. At the same time, Mozambique, Botswana, and Angola would fall, leaving South West Africa and South Africa completely exposed. Rhodesia's northern border is the only hostile one, but it is protected by a natural obstacle, the Zambezi River. The most critical border is that with Mozambique to the east. If the Portuguese lost this territory, it would leave Rhodesia wide open for terrorist invasion. South Africa recognizes this. It is said that when the first landmine explodes on the Umtali–Beira road, South

> Africa will fully intervene.*
>
> It is unlikely that the current terrorist war will stay in the revolutionary stage. There is no classical war threat until a classic war is needed; one *is* needed to take Rhodesia.
>
> It is improbable that the OAU (Organization for African Unity) could mount an invasion, unless with massive Chinese support. Zambia is needed as a base for invasion. Nigeria would supply the most troops, as would Uganda, supported by Libya.

We hope that the Portuguese and South Africans will hold out, but the 'crunch' will come in Rhodesia.

This is why we study and train for classical war. It is expected in the next few years. I must therefore decide in the next few months whether or not to take part in this crucial battle, by committing the next ten years of my life to Rhodesia as an army officer. There is good reason to fight here. In spite of doubt sometimes, I believe this country is worth fighting for. In this decadent age of crisis, I have an opportunity to make a successful career. However, I am not now, nor never have been, really interested in careers, but only in doing what I can for God, family, country, and civilization, thus pursuing my destiny in accordance with God's will.

It seems that staying in the army may be the best way, in spite of the politicians pressing on for majority rule. Although this country, like the United States, is under the influence of international finance, it has not yet lost control of its chances of survival. There is still a possibility of a military coup and popular opposition to majority rule, all of which would give us a fighting chance.

Even if I returned home now, I would be of little value to my family or our cause until I not only complete training, but also have actual combat experience in the field. The future looks bleak indeed for this country, although it is a great country in which to live. Another factor is the explosion here of the African population. There may well be food shortages to come.

This is not to spread alarm and despondency, but only to show the degree of understanding that the military has of Rhodesia's position.

Rhodesians are a great people, and there is much to be optimistic about. Mr

* At the time, John warned that Rhodesia would not get this support. Umtali was later shelled from Mozambique, and history has proved him to be correct.

S.E.D. Brown wrote to me this week. Some of his points are worth quoting: 'The apathy of the average nationalist here is increasing to quite an alarming extent. So many people have just given up fighting ... The big difficulty is that there is not another leader of the stature of Dr Verwoerd to take over'.

The other day, I endeavoured to tell my batman where I came from and where America is on the map. He was so surprised and slapped his cheek, saying, "Ahhh, *baasie*." [Afrikaans for little master].

Yesterday four officer cadets were kicked off the course. Another has left by choice, one has gone AWOL, and two more will also be leaving. Of the original eighteen, twelve now remain. I have survived the first purge.

28 May 1973

The major who gave the lecture on classical war, commented today that the communists work by stages to take over a country. If they are kept from advancing beyond the early stages, they will complete the takeover. One of the best defences is to know the communist plan. In this, he has confidence that Rhodesia can, and will, win its struggle.

The communists plan to conquer Rhodesia by supporting black majority rule for a time. Yet, this is precisely what the Smith government seems to be working toward. Will the officers recognise the internationalist conspiracy at work? The country will be destroyed either way. Will Rhodesians permit this? Will the army, the officers, permit this? It is a political issue, not as military issue.

I began an engineering course today at Brady Barracks in Bulawayo. This is necessary training for defence. The basis of defence is the trench; two- or four-man types, not the big ones of World War I. Trenches have been the basis of defence for the past 200 years.

30 May 1973

One of my instructors, a sergeant major at the School of Military Engineering, said, "The reason you have officers is to do the thinking for the troops."

One evening I was talking with Major Pelham, the chief instructor, about his lecture on the threat of classical war. He said that the terrorist war here is getting more like Vietnam, and that the solution to it is not military, but political. The political solution is to promise eventual majority rule, the same thing promised in terms of the latest settlement proposals with Britain. This, he said, would undermine the whole alleged purpose of the terrorist insurgency. Black rule will be given eventually, instead of immediately. He said that most Rhodesians realize that the ascendency of black power is inevitable because of the sheer force of numbers. They hope, however, that it will be gradual, so that white interest will be maintained. His idea of the role of the military is to "hold back a communist-backed invasion long enough to give the politicians breathing space to make the right decisions, and hope to hell they make the right ones."

This 'political solution', although it ends the *casus belli*, is, in fact, giving in to Rhodesia's enemies and a betrayal of the European civilization here. I don't know if the major's ideas are common to other staff and arms officers in this army, but I can't see them giving much opposition to government policies. The only hope is that the European here will rule his own government and not permit it to give in to internationalist pressures. Otherwise, he will lose the civilization he has built.

2 June 1973

I have completed the first week of a two-week engineering course at Brady Barracks, and it is a very intense one indeed. On Monday and Tuesday we covered trench warfare and obstacles. It is said of conventional warfare, "You dig in or die." We also constructed various wire fences and entanglements, designed not so much to stop the enemy, but to slow him down long enough to hammer him with your fire power.

Another day was spent on the study of the design, construction, and setting of booby traps. We were shown some of Chinese, American and European design. It revealed the barbarism, evil, and madness of very clever and sophisticated minds. One was a flashlight [torch] packed with plastic explosives that would blow your head off when switched on. Most are not intended to kill, but only to maim, so that the victim must be looked after for the rest of his life, instead of just buried and forgotten.

Another two days were spent on demolitions. We were shown how to blow up bridges and buildings, cut steel beams with explosives, and demolish roads and runways. It is a very destructive business, and the force of the explosives is appalling. Demolitions is a very important part of military training, and we spent a whole day practising with the real stuff.

Next week we go on to mine warfare and bridge construction.

6 June 1973

We constructed a rope suspension bridge, and were taught vehicle-flotation. The latter is a simple process of driving a Land Rover onto a tarpaulin, strapping the tarp' on, and lifting the vehicle into deeper water. Remarkably, it works.

Today we laid a minefield. This is the 29th anniversary of the Normandy invasion of Europe by the Allies in World War II. Tonight, we observed the occasion, very appropriately, by staging our own little amphibious landing to breach the minefield. We were divided into three teams, and landed at one and a half hour intervals to clear an eight-yard strip. With a steel rod we had to crawl on our bellies over hard, rocky ground. Every inch of the ground had to be prodded in order to both avoid and to neutralize the mines. It took several hours to cross just a few hundred yards. Along the roads we used an electronic mine detector. This was only practice, but some booby traps were set that let off some charges.

The kit worn by some of the sappers was strange indeed, resembling something from the Hundred Years War of the 14th and 15th centuries. It includes the old British-type helmet worn over a balaclava, and a long prodder which resembles a lance.

7 June 1973

Booby-trapped mines were laid on a road to train us in counter-insurgency warfare. Later we cleared the roads with the help of mine detectors.

16 June 1973

Training resumed this week at its terribly fast pace. Another patrol exercise was held at the Whitewaters Dam near Gwelo. On the second night, I was given command of a fighting patrol to destroy an 'enemy' position. The attack went off well, and I led the patrol to the right place. We crossed the dam in rubber dinghies, hid them, and by compass bearing, came right onto the objective, a big rocky outcrop. I sent the MAG-fire group to one flank, while t took the assault group in a painstakingly crawl on their bellies up the *dwala*. At the top, I fired an Icarus rocket flare to signal the MAG to open fire. The rest of us overran the position, capturing one prisoner. We were, however, surprised by a wire entanglement that tripped-up some of the chaps.

I reorganised the patrol, and we returned to our boats. One course one instructor who had come along as an observer was so incredulous as to the speed of my departure, that he whacked me on the head several times before he could even say what I was doing wrong.

We had to carry a casualty back, but arrived back at the boats without incident. While we were returning across the dam, the main 'enemy' patrol boat fired on us from along the bank. By luck, we had evaded them, and they had not found our boats.

I was complimented for having "an immaculate attack."

Top left: George Coey with his son John on his last day home.

Top right: John, his mother Phyllis and his brother Ed at the airport prior to John's departure for Africa.

Left: Endurance test, Inyanga. A soldier poses next to John's ubiquitous American flag.

Recruit John Lathy grinds it out during the endurance march at Inyanga, May 1972. Note the old .303 training rifle.

John Coey with his favourite accoutrements during the endurance march: a pith helmet and the American flag.

Anthony Kelly posing on the top of World's View, Inyanga, May 1972.

The rugged terrain of World's View, Inyanga.

Sergeant Mason and his dog, May 1972.

Having passed SAS selection are, back row from left: John Coey, John Slatter (from Salisbury) and Dennis Boyd (from Salisbury); and in front Johan Oelofse (from the Orange Free State in South Africa) and Anthony Kelly (from Umtali).

John on the Birchenough Bridge over the Sabi River in the southeast of Rhodesia, May 1972.

Posing in front of a Bedford RL troop-carrier at Cranborne Barracks, Salisbury, May 1972.

John's comrades-in-arms on the Birchenough Bridge, May 1972.

John wearing his pith helmet in front of a Bedford RL, Cranborne Barracks, Salisbury, May 1972.

John writing home, Cranborne Barracks, Salisbury, May 1972.

John poses in front of the statue of Cecil John Rhodes, Jameson Avenue, Salisbury, June 1972.

SAS training, August 1972. George Jenkinson on the left (with the MAG slung) and John Coey on the right (with the FN).

John Coey (at right) with SAS friends in the Zambezi Valley, November 1972.

SAS training at Domboshawa, northeast of Salisbury, August 1972. John Coey is on the left.

B Troop SAS preparing to move out from Gutsa in the Zambezi Valley, November 1972.

SAS canoeing course at Mazoe Dam, north of Salisbury. Oelofse, Jenkinson and Kelly attempt to understand the intricacies of their craft.

The Hunyani Mission church.

SAS passing-out parade, Cranborne Barracks, Salisbury, 15 December 1972. Troopers George Jenkinson and John Alan Coey pose proudly.

Collecting rainwater on an operation in Tete Province, Mozambique, December 1973. Note the well-camouflaged bivouac, or 'bivvy'.

John Coey on patrol in the bush, 1973.

Alouette helicopter uplift in the Zambezi Valley, Tete Province, Mozambique, November 1973.

Above: John Coey at Mount Darwin, June 1975, a month before his death.

Below: RLI soldiers and the Alouette gunner-technician lift a civilian casualty into a G-Car for 'casevac' (casualty evacuation), 1975.

Mount Darwin Fire Force base, 1975. As always, John's American flag has found its way onto a mast.

Lieutenant Joe du Plooy, John Coey's commander during the action when John was killed. Du Plooy was himself later killed in action, in late 1979, when the Puma helicopter he was in was shot down in the Gaza Province of Mozambique.

The Liberty Lobby Bicentennial, Washington D.C., 4 July 1976. From left: Dr Ian Anderson (editor of the Rhodesian *Property and Finance*), Phyllis Coey and Ed Coey.

Corporal Jannie de Beer, killed in action along with John Coey, seen here leading his stick on patrol. *Photo Hannes Wessels*

CHAPTER 17
Defensive Warfare

17 June 1973

I returned to the School of Infantry last week, where training continued in the defensive phase of warfare. The school is one of those places where it is easy to become isolated from the outside world. One becomes so tied up in the intensive study, field exercises, and other commitments.

20 June 1973

This week some very revealing lectures were given. One was on the background of the current terrorist war, of which I have heard nothing since being here. Terrorist organizations ... [censored]. Yesterday afternoon I went over the route and timings with Captain Nick Fawcett BCR, and it was apparent how much he wanted to win it. I saluted him when he finished, more out of respect than formality. I told him we would do our best. He couldn't help but break out into a big smile, showing embarrassment at his display of sentimentality.*

We nearly missed setting the record because my webbing came apart along the route. I also had trouble with my rifle on the range because the gas setting was too high. As a result, and with all the blokes angry and bitching at the end from weariness, I was very upset. I felt like a general who had just lost a battle and was ready to commit suicide. I thought I had let everyone down. Nevertheless, I have a success to my credit.

One of my troubles has been letting my mates take advantage of me. When I am in charge of them, I don't treat them as troopers, but as self-disciplined future officers. The outcome has been that they do not cooperate or work for me as their leader. From the example of the NCOs and officers training us, I can see that I must assert my authority. I need to let my men know who is boss when I take charge of a unit.

I think I should go to the Rhodesian Light Infantry (RLI) when I receive my

* Nicholas Fawcett, was commissioned into the RLI in January 1967, where, in 1970, he was awarded the Bronze Cross of Rhodesia (BCR) for gallantry and leadership in action against a gang of seven terrorists, all of whom were eliminated. He later transferred to the RAR, where his expertise in planning and executing two major operations resulted, in 1977, Nick being made an Officer of the Legion of Merit (OLM).

commission, because Africans have difficulty understanding me. Many think it is better to go to the Rhodesian African Rifles (RAR) first, because they think it is easier to be boss of Africans.*

4 July 1973

Today is the 197th anniversary of American Independence. I marked the occasion by sitting in the bottom of a trench during a defensive exercise. This is trench warfare. It is hard, exhausting work. This trench existence is a severe strain on the soldiers.

6 July 1973

On Wednesday night I experienced a 'jitter patrol', a communist-Chinese technique for destroying morale and the will to resist. It is also used to determine the disposition of a defensive site. We expect this type of attack because of the Chinese influence on the black Marxist ZANLA forces.

Taking a cue from the Marines, I bellowed, "Haw, haw, haw, you bastards, come and get us!" I was, however, told that this was very wrong, since it would give away my position. As a consequence, we were up all night pulling out to another location and digging in again.

After returning from this gruelling exercise, mid-term interviews were given. I was criticized for lack of self-discipline, practical know-how, and lagging interest in the course. This is all true. I have always lacked practical proficiency – a severe handicap, if not disastrous, then for me with the troops.

I let the comments and jibes of my mates get to me, which at times promoted ill feeling between us. I do not have the professional attitude towards my work that an officer should have. All this again makes me reconsider going through with a commission.

7 July 1973

I have been on a defensive exercise to practice trench warfare. This has been an entirely new experience for me, one that I hope will not be repeated often. Trench

* The RLI, formed in 1961, was a regular infantry battalion made up entirely of white men. The much-older RAR, where only the officers are white, served with distinction in both world wars and Malaya.

warfare is a carryover from the world wars, but is still relevant and therefore necessary. It is hard, exhausting work, digging down into hard, sandy ground, filling sandbags, concealing your position, and constructing wire obstacles and laying minefields. Once the trench is dug, you live a miserable, dirty, filthy little existence in a grave-like slot in the ground, from which you move only after dark. That little grave, however, may save your life, for it is the only protection from mortar, artillery and air attack.

One night a 'jitter patrol' was arranged for us, in an attempt to destroy morale by encouraging troops to defect, to give up, or to go home to their wives and families before "you die." Techniques included the playing of popular music to make you homesick, a psychological ploy used by the communists in the Korea War.

The exercise ended with a 'withdrawal'. It is never referred to as a retreat, but is practised as a necessity to reorganize either a defence or a counterattack.

Next Saturday, 14 July, I leave on a tour of the South African Defence Force (SADF). We go by army bus to Pretoria, where we will be flown to various military installations around South Africa. I hope to see my friends while there, but that may be difficult as nearly all our time will be planned.

I have a long weekend off for the Rhodes and Founders national holiday which commemorates the founding of Rhodesia. I notice that, just as in America, national feeling is rarely expressed here, if felt at all. Holidays are just a relief from work. Anyhow, I am recuperating from the exercise and preparing for the trip south. Also, I'm preparing a lecture on American foreign policy, which I hope to present on my return. I intend to expose the Council on Foreign Relations and its role as part of a conspiracy to form a world socialist government. I am anxious to see the reaction.

The tape of General Douglas MacArthur's farewell speech arrived. I am always glad to get letters from home. They are the highpoint of the week.

Enclosed is an article about the mass kidnapping of African school children by Marxist terrorists. This is their 'recruiting' method.*

9 July 1973

Today I drove out to the Zimbabwe Ruins National Park to have a look at the ruins

* On 5 July 1973, ZANLA terrorists abducted 295 staff and pupils from St Albert's Mission in Mount Darwin district. Security forces intercepted the group as it marched towards Mozambique, rescuing all but eight of the abductees.

of an ancient city. The Acropolis and walls are quite impressive structures. The architecture is remarkable when one considers that only regularly-shaped stones were used for construction, with no cementing mixture.

I read of a United States air force colonel who had endured incredible tortures but never broke. When asked what kept him going, he said that four things did: "Discipline, ambition, physical strength, and loyalty to purpose as a military man."

29 July 1973

I am fortunate in taking part in the active defence of this country. A mild level of anti-communism can be found in the country because of the obvious Russian and Chinese threat and their backing of the terrorists. So far, I have met no-one in Rhodesia and few in South Africa who understand anything about the internationalist control of the situation. The one officer who lectured on Zionism and the Middle East was certainly not opposed to it.

The Rhodesian army is not politically inclined, but is, I'm told, much like the old British army. One's personal freedom is greatly restricted, and there is much to endure. Once I finish training, I'll be out in the bush most of the time.

I have a heavy price to pay for coming here, and that is being separated from my family and the country I love most. But, I still feel I must stay on, and that is really for basic survival. South Africa may go the same way as the USA, particularly with its increasing rate of inflation. In time, Rhodesia will also follow.

It is a hard decision to make – whether or not to sell the third decade of my life to an army when the future is so uncertain.

12 August 1973

This week began a new phase of training, also considered part of classical warfare. It is fighting in built-up areas and includes house clearing. It is real movie-type fighting – dashing from house to house and door to door, tossing in grenades, thrusting through doors, and blazing away from the hip. We also performed anti-riot drills. If the army is called on to disperse an illegal assembly, a warning is given to the mob to disperse. If nothing happens, one rioter is picked out and shot, and if that doesn't work, the rest are shot.

This is in anticipation of urban warfare in the African townships, and a likelihood of a Northern Ireland-type disturbance in the future. Also, Matabeleland, the area around Bulawayo, is expected to be the next theatre of activity.

There has been student rioting at the University of Rhodesia in Salisbury. The same old story as back home: blacks protesting discrimination, with the liberal fraternity saying that the police uses too much force and are indiscriminate in their arrests. However, the vice-chancellor of the university warned that if the trouble did not stop, the university would cease to be multiracial.

Next week I give my talk on American foreign policy, plus one on the Watergate scandal. So I have an opportunity to expose our manipulators. I've prepared an eight-page précis on the former and will send it to you. Your comments on Watergate, in past letters, have been most helpful. [The family never received John's paper on American foreign policy.]

Last Friday the commander of the Rhodesian army paid the course a brief visit. He is Lieutenant General Peter Walls, who commanded a small unit of Rhodesian volunteers in Malaya in the 1950s. He told us that in his job he must work closely with the prime minister, his cabinet, and other high-ranking government officials. He added that whenever things are going well in the terrorist war, they all try to be generals. But when things go wrong, they expect him to have all the answers. Smith, he said, unlike some government people, is behind the army all the way, and that is a big help.

15 August 1973

Today I gave a lecture on American foreign policy, in the hope of revealing the ultimate enemy to the officer cadets and officers who must contend with the workings of the internationalist conspiracy in their daily lives as soldiers. I explained how the United States has, in fact, built its own enemy, and how the Council of Foreign Relations controls the United States government and its policies. This has given me a chance to expose our real enemy as well as to state my case for coming to Rhodesia.

16 August 1973

This morning I lectured on the Watergate affair.

17 August 1973

This afternoon a Presbyterian padre spoke to us on the role of the Christian in the

Rhodesian army. He revived my lagging sense of purpose and faith in these people. He reminded us that the Rhodesians were holding the line for Western civilization in the Zambezi Valley. Although most of the soldiers are non-Christian, the people secular and the politicians are subjected to external influences detrimental to the welfare of the state. It is Western civilization that makes Christianity a religion that can be practised openly and freely. If Rhodesia ceases to be Western, Christianity will become an underground religion.

All the present terrorist incursions are directed against the white form of government, with the result that several white farmers have been killed or attacked. But it is largely the Africans who have suffered. Many who do not cooperate with the terrorists have been tortured and killed, and their cattle slaughtered. The army has the Christian role of the strong defending the defenceless. Many claim that the terrorist war is a result of UDI (Unilateral Declaration of Independence of 11 November 1965), but it began long before then.

Like many of my American contemporaries and peers, I have attempted to find purpose and meaning in life. I have found it, although I still get confused and don't have all the answers.

Although a new army may be built in America, it will still be an instrument of a corrupt, power-hungry conspiracy. [Remainder censored]

19 January 1973

In my two lectures on American foreign policy and Watergate, I used the opportunity to expose the internationalist conspiracy as the cause behind Rhodesia now having to fight a border war.

I also explained how the United States had built its own enemy, and is controlled by the CFR. This coincided very nicely with my talk on Watergate, which I could only explain as I have seen it so far: a further drive to overthrow the Republic by destroying the check-and-balance system, and also, a power struggle manipulated by the CFR oligarchy in an attempt to shift personnel within the Republican Party. At any rate, I had a very attentive audience, and many were shocked. My précis is being distributed within the army, so I feel I have scored a success.

I know from my past acquaintances in the ROTC and US Marine Corps, and from reading US army journals we get over here, that many in the American forces have attempted to find meaning in life. They have turned to the doctrine of 'professionalism' to rebuild a demoralized army, something which has nearly become an obsession. I'm all for professionalism, but they have not found the moral purpose that American forces once had, whether real or imagined.

Whether or not I get commissioned, I will serve here for the minimum term of five years. I cannot leave until I have taken part in the fight. I will have accumulated enough leave to come home for a few months in 1975. These are decisive years, but if the country falls, all commitments would be void.

After three days of written and practical exams this week, we are off on a week-long classical war exercise, starting on Friday. This will end the second term, which will be followed by fourteen days off. I am going to Lake Kariba for three days with one of my mates. After that I will be going down to Pretoria.

An article in the *Rhodesia Herald* newspaper of 15 August claims that allegations of Portuguese massacres are communist inventions cooked up in Prague under Russian supervision. Although credible. Mai Lai-type stories are concocted by the Czech secret service and the KGB, to 'focus attention on the evils of Western Imperialism in the Third World'.

31 August 1973

I have finished a seven-day classical war exercise in the Ngezi National Park area, where we covered, at company and battalion level, various phases of defence, demolition, guard, attack, and withdrawal. I held various posts as platoon sergeant and commander, as well as understudy commander for the company and battalion. This has provided me with an opportunity to examine both myself and the army more thoroughly. I have successfully led a platoon during which I received the cooperation of my men, but I often take too long in reacting and sorting out situations. I know I can do the job.

I am impressed by the ability of some of the officers in their positions of command.

CHAPTER 18
Counter-Insurgency Warfare (COIN)

2 September 1973

I have finished the second phase of training and managed to survive a week of exams as well as the classical war exercise. I am spending a few days in Salisbury in the home of one of my fellow cadets, before going down to Bulawayo, and then on to Pretoria. I won't be going to Kariba after all, because the people I had planned to stay with there were all killed last week in a vehicle accident in South Africa.

I am going to revise the précis I wrote on American foreign policy, so that I can see if I can get it printed in the army magazine *Assegai.* I am going to work on it over my break. I am sure Mr S.E.D. Brown can assist me in this. Also the people with whom I've been staying work for a magazine called *Illustrated Life Rhodesia*, and they may help me to get it printed in that, under a pseudonym, of course. Next term from mid-September to December, we cover counter-insurgency warfare (COIN), which is what is being fought here now. This will finally determine if I stay on or not. Even if I do not get a commission, I would, of my own choice, go back to the SAS to serve at least another year.

7 September 1973

I've been given fourteen days' leave, and have gone to Salisbury and Bulawayo, where I have stayed in the homes of my fellow course members. I stopped at the Anglican Cathedral in Salisbury to renew my dedication to purpose and the will of God.

Whenever I see the Browns, I get a better picture of the political scene over here. After a long period of blackout treatment, Brown and the *South African Observer* are receiving a lot of adverse publicity in the press. They are also being attacked by both Vorster and liberal Afrikaners alike.

I will be having another letter printed in the October issue of the *South African Observer.* I also rewrote the paper on American foreign policy, hoping to have it printed in *Assegai*, but that remains to be seen.

In July, I wrote a letter to my US congressman, pointing out how strategic Rhodesia and South Africa are to the West, how they are preventing a communist takeover, and how they need his support in legislation before Congress. He sent back a very nice reply, thanking me, and writing that he 'would keep my comments in mind'. I'm sure he would say the same if I had urged the United States to bomb Salisbury.

The upcoming term is most important as well as very interesting, as it deals with COIN, or revolutionary, warfare. This lasts until Christmas time. We will be doing a tracking and survival course later on. We will also be participating in real war.

The term started with training in COIN warfare. This week we covered troop movements, counter-ambush drills, and the setting up of basecamps. I do not feel very confident about all of this, and am having second thoughts about the whole matter. I am tempted to go back to the SAS to serve out my time as a soldier in the ranks, as I have grave doubts about my leadership ability under the conditions of the Zambezi Valley. The heat makes me idle and complacent.

This term will be decisive for me, and will determine whether I go for an infantry officer's commission, or go back to the ranks, or maybe even leave the army completely. I'm afraid that if I do leave the army, and perhaps start working in a civilian job, my whole purpose for living will be destroyed. This would mean that all the work I've done since coming to Rhodesia would have been for nothing.

I feel close to failure, simply because I do not think or react fast enough. This may be my undoing. As one officer cadet said, "It makes one question the very foundation of his leadership and manhood."

I pray to God to restore my self-confidence and help me to overcome my self-doubts. Once again, in this time of need, I have nowhere to turn but to God.

I do not want to become a soldier or an officer for its own sake, but only because, by doing so, I can accomplish my mission in life fighting for Christian civilization and against its enemies. I ask only for success in doing that in my lifetime.

There has been a victory for the West: the overthrow of the Marxist government in Chile by a military junta … [censored]. I've prepared a presentation on revolutionary warfare, or COIN, for a parents' day this weekend. I've stressed the communist motivation behind it, and the four phases of 'national liberation':

1. Preparatory phase: infiltration and recruiting for the revolution.
2. Active resistance phase: coercion, terrorism, subversion to neutralize the opposition, and to gain support for the revolution.

3. Insurgency phase: guerrilla warfare and the establishment of a revolutionary government.
4. Counter-offensive phase: the revolution assumes the part of a people's war against the government.

The outcome depends on who gets the support of the masses.

5 October 1973

This past week has been spent in the training of educational techniques: how to teach and train soldiers. For practical work, I have a lecture on fire-control orders, and organised a lecture and demonstration on the safe handling of weapons. In this army, an officer must train his men in every aspect of soldiering and, God willing, I want command of a troop or platoon. This will be a real challenge for me to make an efficient fighting force.

I met the officer commanding Regimental Wing, a Major Davy, who inspired me. He said that Rhodesia could win its war overnight if the decision would be made to attack and destroy terrorist rear bases in black Africa, even in Tanzania, and to strike the strategic areas where the power cliques are concentrated. The greatest mistake of the African nations is their belief that they are immune from counterattack.

Africa, he said, is a brutal continent, where only power is understood. It has only ever been superficially civilized. The African has no word for loyalty, although some may be loyal. The majority Mashona ethnic group should be eternally grateful to the European for saving them from extermination by the Matabele in the 1890s.

Africa is like an inflated paper bag waiting to be burst, if not by the Africans themselves, then by the Chinese.

The Rhodesian army is a crack force, and is very critical of itself. It is successful even though it has hardly any resources. The army must work hard to transform the citizen force into fighting soldiers.

Part of the tragedy of Rhodesia is that the Europeans consider the British as the enemy, and rightly so. The breakdown of the Federation of Rhodesia and Nyasaland and its dissolution at the end of 1963, together with UDI, created this rift between Rhodesian and Briton. The quality of loyalty has caused great dissension, especially amongst officers, for some say that if Britain attacked Rhodesia, however unlikely that may be, they would not order their men to fire on British soldiers. Many officers sold their loyalties to the highest bidder at the breakup of the Federation.

If the whole of the SAS was dropped into Zambia and Tanzania to knock out an instillation or assassinate a power group, and even if none returned to Rhodesia, the regiment would have fulfilled its purpose for being.

Major Davy claims that the time is coming when soldiers will rule the world, bringing order and authority to the chaos, anarchy, and decay of the era. Shades of Sulla and Augustus.

Rhodesians must go for strategic points such as terrorist training camps, and not just for kills.

6 October 1973

The past two weeks have been very busy for us here. Much time is spent on training how to lay an ambush, which is one method that achieves the most enemy kills. Last Saturday was open day for parents, and it went off very well. My presentation was very impressive and dramatic, but my point may have been lost, as I'm afraid that most found it more entertaining than informative.

It is well into October, and the year is slipping away quickly. It is very hot now, and the rainy season has started. The jacaranda trees are blooming, leaving the streets and parks covered with violet and blue carpets of blossoms. Many birds are in magnificent plumage colours of orange, green and yellow. But there is still nothing that can compare with our trees back home when the leaves change their colour in autumn.

10 October 1973

Yesterday and last night I participated in an ambush exercise. It became apparent how much planning goes into even simple operations if they are to succeed.

Since coming on this course, military subjects have become my main concern, displacing many others that once held my interest. Today an education officer attempted to discuss topical subjects, but I had nothing intelligent to say about them. I didn't really care either. Command of troops is my main objective now, to prove myself, and once and for all to consolidate my action and purpose in coming here. I can back up my ideas with action. I can do it all.

11 October 1973

It was brought to my attention today that the article I submitted to *Assegai* magazine is considered 'subversive', not because it is anti-Rhodesian or criticizes the state here, but because it "destroys misconceptions about America being pro-Western, and may lower morale of read by the general public." Although what I have written is true, it is feared that the public may not be able to stand the truth. The facts I have presented may make the article appear anti-American to those who do not understand how America is ruled by the CFR oligarchy, whose interest is total world power.

I hold my country and its people dear, and hope for the salvation of their freedom.

The opportunity of going into the Rhodesian Education Corps is now definitely open to me. I would attend the University of Rhodesia for several months to get a teaching diploma. Then I would be assigned instructional tasks in current affairs, military history, English grammar, and many other subjects. I could do much, I think, toward seeing that the army knows the truth, while at the same time fulfilling my desire to become an educator.

First, however, I want to go to the infantry to do my part of the fighting in the bush, for the honour of my family as well as a moral obligation. I believe that God has given me the opportunity to accomplish everything I want to do. My life and future are in His hands.

I conducted a training exercise for the other cadets on how to handle the MAG under field conditions. It was successful, showing that I have progressed to a stage where I can now instruct. I seem to be a very practical person, and this course has greatly increased my abilities.

My course instructor rebuked me the other day for wearing an old-style bush hat during the ambush exercise. He remarked, significantly, that I was a Rhodesian. I wonder if he realized what he had said.

19 October 1973

I have just completed a week-long battle camp at a place called Mambo Hills in Matabeleland, a rugged mountainous area north east of Bulawayo. It is similar to the Matopos, a fantastic place with lots of caves and caverns which provide excellent hideouts.

We practised battle skills such as snap-shooting at pop-up targets, skirmishing, and shooting at unseen targets in likely cover. We trained for patrolling, encounter actions, ambushing, and tracking down terrorists on follow-ups.

The day before, when we were to attack a 'terr' camp, I managed to walk right into it and was fired upon. This compromised our security, so consequently, when the attack was put in, the 'enemy' was no longer there. I led the follow-up to track down the 'enemy', encountered them, and no doubt would have lost several men had the fight been real. The lesson learned was that I would have caused needless deaths through my carelessness. Follow-ups are dangerous. A night attack is much more lethal to the terrs.

I was so upset at the time that I was ready to give up the infantry. God forbid that I ever repeat any of these mistakes.

20 October 1973

The best news this week has been a seventy percent pay increase for all servicemen. So I'll be getting about fifty dollars a month extra. So happy is the day when the army gets its pay. It's about time too. Soldiers are about the lowest paid in the country, but even with the pay increases, the pay is still below equivalent civilian levels. I can't help but wonder if this is a foreboding of inflation.

I am happy to see my letter printed in this month's *South African Observer.*

Next week we train for urban insurgency, riot control, and cordon-and-search operations. We do another week-long exercise for practice, which should all be very interesting.

CHAPTER 19
Disappointment, Betrayal and Persecution

24 October 1973

There has been a very sudden turn of events. Another chap and I have been removed from the officers' course. My removal is supposedly for the reason that I do not have the 'academic qualifications and the temperament' needed to be an officer. So ends another phase of my army career. The question is what to do next?

There is no purpose in going into forestry work available in Bulawayo. I cannot go home yet because my mission here is incomplete. There is still much to learn. I must gain the battle experience that will enable me to help people so that when the time comes, they are able to counter the revolution.

I must go back to the SAS and serve as a trooper, although it means risking getting killed in the war. It is the one course open to me to fulfil my desire of serving God, family, country, and preserve civilization here. I would be of no use or help if I returned home now. I am sure all this is part of God's plan for my life.

I have not failed, and the time spent here at the school has not been wasted. I have increased my capabilities a great deal. I could have been a platoon commander. I was surprised and disappointed at this turn of events, but not sorry. I feel I have contributed to the course by helping those who will receive their commissions next year. It is the final answer that I've sought for months now.

I am returning to Salisbury today, so write to my old address. I don't think you will be disappointed, but it is just the way things have turned out. I may be mad for staying on, but I cannot do otherwise. God bless you all.

[censored] … accomplished his mission, but victory, victory, victory, is the alternate objective, and victory is achieved through prayer. I was glad I shook up a few people. The trouble is that most people do not believe in what they are fighting for. They do not have faith in their civilization. Although it may have its faults, it is certainly one of the finest in the world. People are not convinced of the justification of their cause.

28 October 1973

It has occurred to me that I may have been 'had'. Major Busby and others in the

Education Corps had accepted me into that unit, yet at my last interview, I was told that "although the course officers attempted to place you there, your qualities could not be used."

Who decided? Army headquarters? Is it because my article to *Assegai* was considered subversive? Is it because of the truth in my lectures? Is it because someone knew about my articles in the *South African Observer* and decided to give me the chop? I don't know how to find out.

The reasons I was given may have been true, as yes, there were shortcomings on my part, but were they really sufficient to warrant my removal from the course? Perhaps I should have heeded the warnings about using my name in the articles I wrote.

Reflecting back on the events of the week, I think it is good that I left the officer training programme. All during the course I sacrificed my individuality by trying to conform to what the course training personnel wanted me to be. I had to become completely obedient to the whims of the system, the establishment, and a power-hungry little course officer.

If I had been commissioned, I would have been drawn into pursuing a career, becoming completely obedient to appease the establishment. Now, as a trooper, I once again have control of my destiny, albeit just as a little cog in a big wheel.

It is a game of who is using whom. The army and government use me as a pawn, yet I am using the army to fulfil my hopes and desires. I think I am getting the most.

Although we are all wary of the politicians, they are backing the military, giving it considerable freedom – a freedom that is just short of all-out invasion of the north. Even that may come in the course of time. Never forget the army here is holding the line for Western civilization, a very real purpose. I've been blessed to take part in it. Dangerous? Yes, but it is something all of us have to do sometime, and I can do it with one of the best units in which one can serve, commission or not.

I've moved to Salisbury now, back to Cranborne Barracks. I have been posted to 2 Section of A Troop. I am repeating my ground training for parachuting, since I have not jumped since January. I'll be jumping again this week.

In a couple of weeks, I'll be going on operations in the north-eastern border area the Zambezi. Now all the training I've had will be put to use.

My posting hasn't changed my plans for going home on leave in 1975. I'll be finished in the army in 1977.

As for suggestions for Christmas, you can always send over tapes of classical music. Today I bought two tapes, one of Strauss Waltzes and the other Beethoven's *Ninth Symphony*. It is really a pleasure to listen to them. If you can find them, I'd really like to hear the Slavonic dances, and the *Love Theme* from *Ben Hur.* There is nothing else I really need. God bless you all.

29 October 1973

Although only a trooper, or 'jarhead', I can fight my own war against the establishment of socialist one-worlders, the true revolutionaries.

2 November 1973

I've had a grand week, revising on my para-training and enjoying four jumps at New Sarum air force base. I feel parachuting is both a sport and an occupational skill in which I can become proficient.

I've had a hard week reconciling myself to the squadron and to my status. For the next few years I must forget about becoming an officer. I've had a good look at what that entails, and perhaps it is better to start at the lowest rank, to work up, and to gain experience, before leading men to their deaths. I will have the advantage of seeing both aspects of an officer and an enlisted man.

I believe that what my section commander said may be true: "It is better to be a sergeant than an officer." I can still accomplish my mission in this country as a trooper.

3 November 1973

Although I cannot prove anything yet, I feel the real reason for my demise as an officer cadet is the article I wrote for the *Assegai* magazine. As I said before, it is considered subversive, even though it has nothing to do with Rhodesia or its government. It had already been decided that I would go into the Education Corps, but I think it was an army headquarters decision that I should be purged. They may have thought that if I could write about the American government in that way, then I could do the same about the Rhodesian government, which is true.

Should things go against me too much, I can always catch the next flight away, but I would not like to do that.

I'll be going out to the bush on 14 November. I hope this will be north of the Zambezi. This is what I want, for we will be protecting one of the last of the European overseas empires from communist invasion, and with it, the advance of barbarism.

We are going north.

I've sent some parcels over. One is a photograph of the squadron taken last December at my passing-out parade.

Next week I'll be doing more parachute jumps, as well as preparing for the bush. Don't worry; my life is in God's hands. It is good being back in Salisbury, and to renew old acquaintances. It is much livelier that in Gwelo.

Now that I am off the officers' course, I have had time to think and reflect on what I am doing and what I am living for. If I were not a Christian, I would be a good communist, for we think and believe in much the same way – only if different directions.

We see the world in crisis due to the impact of science and technology on mankind. They have eliminated belief in the supernatural and faith in God. The result has been world wars, world depression, and world desperation. Communists believe the world must be changed, and so do I. The communists have a faith and a vision that inspire them. It is a faith in man as the creative intelligence of the world. They believe that by the force of his rational intelligence, man can redirect his destiny and reorganize his life and the world. By denying God, man becomes the most intelligent. The communists believe that because man's mind is the most decisive force in the world, there is no need for God. Man's mind is man's fate. Communists use insurrection and … [censored].

10 November 1973

This is the last weekend before I do my first five-week tour of duty on the north-eastern border, referred to here as the 'sharp end'. It is a long weekend since Monday is Rhodesia's independence day.

It is time to do what I came here for, to destroy a monster created by some of my own countrymen. It threatens to destroy the civilization here, one which I think is good, but it lacks culture. The old cry of 'For God and Country' lingers on in this former British colony, and in the last of the colonial empires, Portugal's overseas territories. The advance of communism and conspiracy must be stopped, both on the ground and in the world capitals. I must first do the former, then move on to the other.

I am going to donate the large American flag you sent me to the Anglican Cathedral in Salisbury. There are many old flags there, including Union Jacks, and military ones such as Queen's colours and old battle flags. I think enough Americans have contributed to this fight to warrant putting up the Stars and Stripes as a token. I must first write a memorandum for the dean of the cathedral, so that he will understand the significance of the gift. He will then present the case to the church council and board of elders. Somehow, I think it will be accepted. Could you send over another American flag?

There is an American missionary family here from South Dakota. Their son, a good friend of mine, has gone back to the States to join the air force. They are soon going over for his wedding, and will stay for several months. They are rather naïve people, but I enjoy visiting them as they are thoroughly dedicated Christians. They have had me in their home for dinner.

I met a girl from Hamilton, Ohio, who is here for four years to work for a mission society. It is really good to talk to someone who knows the old home state and has been to the same places that I have.

I'm still friends with the Jenkinsons, but I don't see them very often. The last time was in September when they came up to the open day at the school. George was truly sorry to see me leave.

I'll record a tape for you before I head out to the frontier. Don't worry about me. I figure if God intends for me to get killed there, then there is nothing else for me to do in this world. I'll be back in Salisbury before Christmas, but I don't know when I'll get my next letter off. So I'll close wishing you a happy Thanksgiving.

12 November 1973

The following is sung by the paratroopers to the tune of *The Red River Valley*:

> When the green light comes on we are ready,
> For the sergeant to shout, Number One.
> When we stand on the plane altogether,
> We will all tumble out one by one.

So come sit by your drinks and be merry,
Drink a toast to those men of the sky.
Here's a toast to those men dead already.
And a toast to those men still to die.

When we land in a far distant country,
There's a job we will do very well.
We will blow up old ZAPU and ZANU,
And all of those commies as well.

CHAPTER 20
23rd Birthday and Bush Patrols

12 November 1973

Today is my twenty-third birthday. Yesterday, 11 November, was the eighth anniversary commemorating independence day for Rhodesia.

I have been busy making my peace with God and with many people I know in Salisbury, before doing my tour of duty beginning later this week – just in case I get drilled [shot].

I told several people in church that, although I appreciated their prayers for the safety and well-being of the servicemen on duty, I am disappointed that no-one ever prays for victory. Whether the soldier lives or dies is not really as important, but it is victory that makes his service worthwhile and meaningful. A soldier in battle will have ... [censored].

The other patrols have contacted terrorists and have captured an AK47 rifle – a great victory. Our turn must be coming soon. I hope, but dread.

The sky is so blue, the sun so brilliant, the forests of mopane so green, the ground so hard, the waters so sweet, the breeze so refreshing, the swarms of mopane flies so annoying – buzzing in one's ears, eyes and nostrils.*

There is a beautiful caterpillar I've seen frequently. It has an orange head, black body with yellow stripes, red splotches white spots. Its chrysalis is brilliant scarlet.

I was thrilled last night when, for the first time, I heard an elephant trumpet.

23 November 1973

Our mission has been changed. Now we must go back to our starting point for resupply and to check out a terrorist basecamp. We have been lucky so far, having no contacts. God has been with us, supplying water daily. We feel we are in for it now. Sooner or later we will find them. No-one seems terribly eager to close with and destroy the enemy. So, after reaching a riverbed, now dry, that may well be a terrorist supply route into Rhodesia, we go back.

* Although commonly called a mopane fly, it is actually a very small stingless bee, *Plebeina hildebrandti*, which is drawn to moisture, the human face offering a ready source.

24 November 1973

We are to reconnoitre a big terr camp that had been attacked before, but may still be in use. We left the hot springs and carried on over burned ground and gravelly hills. We stopped by a water point, nearly exhausted, in a near-tropical place along a river, with palm trees and thick bamboo growth. The intense heat and humidity quickly saps one's strength on the marches. Once again, I thank and praise God that water has been found.

What a primitive existence, hunting terrs and water, hiding in cover, and occasionally washing yourself and your clothes when there is sufficient water. It is going back to nature. It is unlike anything I've ever done before. All sophisticated airs of city life are dropped, and I can see why primitive people worship gods of sun, rain, water, and the like. What a life, with a rifle always by your side.

26 November 1973

We have rested a day during which we were resupplied by airdrop from a Dakota with provisions for another ten days of patrolling. Each of us got a tin of fresh orange juice and a beer. We moved back down to the waterhole, and will proceed to the OP [observation point] over the terrorist camp.

The patrol commander gave us a bullying for being 'switched off' and warned that we would 'come short' sometime. It is so hot, and the burden so heavy, especially now after our resupply. One has difficulty concentrating.

While patrolling, we march a few thousand metres in the morning, stop at water and shade during the heat of the day, then move off again in the afternoon. The radio must be set up at 1600 hours. Supper is cooked an hour or so before last light. After dark, we move off again, just in case we were seen. Then we bivouac for the night in a tight little circle, sit and listen, and, one by one, lay out our bedrolls and settle for sleep. We take turns at guard duty.

I think, perhaps, that after this tour in the bush I will have done my job here. Or is there more to be done?

The energy crisis, beginning to be felt in Rhodesia, is being used to increase the dictatorial powers of the American government.

My brother suggest the possibility that I was kicked off the officers' course and sent to the front for 'liquidation', like Uriah the Hittite was by King David. I like the comparison, yet my so-called subversive article was published and accepted by the army as true. Do I have unseen political enemies, as some friends suggest, whom I will never know or see?

27 November 1973

We have returned to the airstrip and are sitting on a *gomo* above it, overlooking a valley. I am in a little fortress of rocks, with my thin green *bivvy* giving me shade and cover from rain. Far off I hear thunder, but the sun continues to shine brightly. Water is plentiful, and I feel secure in God's grace and blessing. Friendly lizards gaze at me from their perches on black and grey boulders. Colourful butterflies settle on my legs or arms and lap the salty sweat with their proboscises. All is so pleasant here. Looking down over the scene below me, the troubles of the world seem far away. News I do not want. Yet, this is a war we are fighting, although, after eleven days, we have not seen a terr or civilian.

28 November 1973

This morning we joined up with two other patrols at a terrorists basecamp called Kuhari (pronounced 'coo-ar-ee'). The place had been deserted by all Africans. We found benches, tables, bicycles, pots, huts made of bamboo, and cleared fields. No doubt, they will be back after we're gone. Terrs depend on rural Africans for support, so the terrs' supply lines into Rhodesia extend from kraal to kraal. So the only way to solve the problem is to remove all the Africans from the area. What a hot and humid place this is. The cleared fields quickly revert back into forest.

29 November 1973

Yesterday afternoon five terrs fired into our camp from higher ground. It woke everyone up from the complacency of the previous days. This morning we located a very large enemy basecamp, with many thatched huts and food-storage bins. It may be the relocated Kuhari we went through yesterday. We advanced in an extended line, ready for action, but again, the camp had been evacuated, probably only the day before. The terrs left huts, straw baskets, water gourds, and four dogs. We simply left the place as we had found it, although I felt we should have destroyed the huts. Much effort had gone into the camp, but in counter-insurgency the only success is in enemy kills. Our terrs are still at large, but on the run, so may well have a squirt at us again.

Today is Thanksgiving Day at home, and I thank God for the limited success we had today. The water party was ambushed by two terrs with AKs. No-one was hurt, thank God. The SAS escapes again.

30 November 1973

We moved up on a high mountain for an OP, from where we could see the Zambezi in the far distance. We stopped for a resupply of water by air then moved off again. A mug of strong, sweet coffee never tasted better. We are moving towards another terr basecamp, one on which all patrols will converge.

1 December 1973

This morning the now-combined patrols searched for another terr basecamp, but found nothing. We then went up a *gomo* for another OP. Dear God, send some rain, for we are running out of water again, and it's so hot. We sit in our meagre shade and sweat and doze and sweat.

I've decided to try to go home on leave in a few months. I intend making use of this time to see how things are there, and to decide if Rhodesia will be my home or not. I remember this time two years ago, standing by the Hide Away Hills golf course at home, in a burst of warm rays of winter sun. How I want to go back and see it all just once more. God help me do it and help me endure all this.

Rain clouds are moving in again. A wind blows strong, then dies, then comes again. One hears thunder.

I feel so tired, energy sapped, and useless now. I've lost interest in the operation and just don't care where we go or what we do, just as long as we get water soon. It has started to rain just a bit, and everyone has set out their *bivvies* in an attempt to catch rainwater. What a sight. But the rain stopped all too quickly to be of any real benefit.

3 December 1973

The patrols split up, and we were choppered many kilometres to the east, over endless miles of forests. What a ride. The entire patrol is down with diarrhoea, no doubt from the water we had to drink. We are not sure where we are.

5 December 1973

Two members of the patrol were casevaced yesterday … [censored].

The following letter home was written over several days in December 1973:

I have just returned to Salisbury, after twenty-nine days on reconnaissance patrols in the western province of Mozambique, called Tete. We were in an area which we knew nothing about because the Rhodesian security forces had not been there for a long time. We came here to find out about terrorist activity in this subverted area, and to locate bases and supply routes into Rhodesia. There are no actual roads or trails such as the Ho Chi Minh Trail in Vietnam. Weapons and supplies are taken by the terrs from kraal to kraal, while food is taken from locals through intimidation. I personally believe the locals, far from being active sympathisers and supporters of Frelimo,* would prefer just to be left alone by the terrorists, both Portuguese and Rhodesian.

Counter-insurgency operations cannot be successful unless all locals are evacuated from the area. This, the Portuguese have attempted with their *aldeamentos*, or camps. These are fenced-in compounds, surrounded by cultivated lands. They are fortified with trenches and wire. They are guarded by militia, surrendered Frelimo terrorists who wear black uniforms and berets. There may also be a few Portuguese. The purpose of these camps is to deny local support to the terrs, or, in Mao's terminology, 'to deny the sea to the fish'. The Rhodesians are trying to use these in the north-east districts now†

The *aldeamentos* are a successful means of control, but it is very difficult to round up all the local people over such a vast area. It results most of the cultivated fields having to be abandoned and to revert to bush, which is a reverse of the development which the Portuguese had hoped to accomplish in their colonies. As the war escalates, many settlements,

* Frelimo, from the Portuguese *Frente de Libertação de Moçambique*, the Front for the Liberation of Mozambique, was the guerrilla movement fighting to overthrow Portuguese control of the colony. They were very active against the Portuguese military in the Tete province, a region adjacent to the whole of Rhodesia's north-eastern border, and therefore also a key infiltration route for ZANLA insurgents into Rhodesia.

† Rhodesia would emulate this strategy, constructing hundreds of 'protected villages' throughout the north-eastern and eastern operational border areas.

African and European, have been abandoned, and locals have taken to the hills. It is a shame, as this could be a highly-productive area.

Portuguese authorities have permitted Rhodesian troops to operate in Tete since the beginning of the year. The SAS has conducted several operational jumps there since the beginning of 1972. Operations are primarily reconnaissance patrols, such as I've been on, to locate the enemy.

We found three camps, Kuhari, Moses and Rudodo. Airstrikes called on some. Three patrols joined up to go through Kuhari, advancing in extended line, weapons ready, adrenaline pumping. But the camp had been abandoned shortly before.

All the terr camps are African settlements, which makes it difficult to tell apart terrorists from civilians. We captured two suspects, and sent them back to our headquarters basecamp for interrogation.

The question in everyone's mind is if operations like this are worthwhile, or are they just a waste of time? Is this another no-win war like Vietnam?

Operations of this type are primarily of a preventive nature. Earlier this year, much of this area was dominated by terrorists who were very secure here. Since the SAS has been working the area, the terrs have been unbaled to establish themselves or subvert an area.*

The enemy, knowing the army are present, flee, for they are scared, even though they may fire quick bursts or a few mortars before taking off. Success, therefore, is not in the number of enemy dead or an objective destroyed, but in stopping the revolution in its early phases, before it expands. In this sense we were successful. A first step towards victory, although it is not always apparent. Morale at times really drops. It is so easy to lose interest. Often there is no desire at all to close in and destroy the enemy. Many just don't care.

* The SAS later referred to their presence in Mozambique as the Macombe Days. In September 1973, the SAS established a tactical headquarters in an *aldeamento* at Macombe, just south of the Zambezi River. It had its own airstrip, which was a big advantage. Patrols were deployed by parachute, operating in an area for six weeks, ambushing, observing, and seeking out ZANLA terrorist camps. Regarded by many as one of the most successful counter-insurgency operations of the Rhodesian bush war, the SAS went on to patrol north of the Zambezi, leaving freshly-deployed elements of the RAR to keep the area south of the river clear of the enemy. Conditions were extremely harsh for the SAS troops, far away from their own country and families, soldiering in hostile countryside which the enemy had liberally festooned with anti-personnel mines. This external operation lasted well over a year.

CHAPTER 21
A Parachute Jump

What is an operation like? The jump is very exciting. Troopers with blackened faces wait in the dimmed lights of the aircraft for the command, "Action station." It seems that you stand for hours in agony, with the weight of your kit and container strapped to your leg. You are only too glad to jump when "Go" is given.

The wind whips you away from the aircraft and the roar of its engines, as you float down in ghostly silence. The stick of soldiers strings out across the sky. Those that jumped out first are below you, and those who left after you, are above you.

To the south, the moon reflects on the Zambezi and illuminates the forest canopy below with soft silvery light. The wind swings you around in a spiral, so that you cannot tell how and where exactly you will land. Some land in trees and have to release their reserve 'chutes to climb down, while others crash through to the ground. Much time is spent trying to locate one another in the dark. Some are not found until morning. We move off to the landing zone where we were supposed to have landed. Parachutes and equipment are gathered up and concealed for later recovery. Now each patrol heads for its assigned territory.

Having covered a few kilometres in the morning, the patrol stops to cook and rest during the heat of the day. In the afternoon it sets off again. When it gets dark, we bed down in a little circle, everyone taking a turn at guard duty.

The heat and humidity quickly sap one's strength and energy. You hope and pray for water and rain to relieve the miseries of patrolling: the burning sun, the aching muscles, the parched throat, and the swollen tongue. Water means life. The heat kills your appetite. We consume tea and health foods mostly. A man loses ten to fifteen pounds through profuse sweating.

But there are the simple pleasures of the primitive existence: the blue sky, the occasional cooling breeze, the sweet taste of water when found, the brilliant sunsets, the starlit night skies, the barking baboons, and the thrill of a jumbo trumpeting.

The first ten days are the worst, for that is when one misses the city and its attractions most. After that one becomes accustomed to the loneliness and routine. Resupply comes every ten days. The fresh meat, beer, and mail dropped in relieve the situation.

One goes for days without seeing a trace of human habitation, but there is always the threat and thrill of an ambush that shatters the silence and complacency, with the rattle of AKs and machine guns. It is a struggle to stay alert in the heat.

One's concept of time changes. Evenings and mornings come and go, a week passes, and time merges into one big memory. Finally, one morning the order comes over the radio, "Find an LZ, (pronounced L-Zed – a landing zone for the helicopter top land in) you will be choppered out at 1100 hours."

Morale skyrockets, grins split faces from ear to ear, and the first laughter in days is heard. Hats soar skyward. At the appointed time the chopper lifts off, giving a bird's eye view of the mountains, rivers and forests we have patrolled. We sweep over *aldeamentos* and fields. Flying low over the Zambezi River a hippo splashes in fright.

Later a Dakota airlifts us from HQ basecamp on the Zambezi to Salisbury. The men are jubilant. They take one last look as the plane passes over the escarpment into Rhodesia. Farewell to the savannah, the baobabs, the Zambezi – farewell.

We've been given a week off over Christmas, during which I will be staying in Salisbury. I've been invited to spend the day at the homes of several people. I haven't yet decide what to do but, in the meantime, I'm just taking it easy.

I may be leaving the SAS soon for posting to another corps. Where or when, I don't know, but these two years with the infantry have been enough, even if much of the time was spent in training. Training, however, is often harder than field service.

I am going to try and get a couple of months' leave in 1974, perhaps around August or October, so that I can go home for a while. I want to see how it is before deciding if I should go back home permanently or to stay here.

I met a Christian evangelist and told her the whole story of my coming here, including my demise from the officers' course and the SAS. At first I didn't want to tell her anything, but, somehow, it all came out as something of a confession. This really hurt my pride. Yet, it relieved a burden. She assured me that it is God's will, and that I must trust in him.

Thank you very much for the tape of Pastor Lang's Thanksgiving service. It is good to again hear the bells, chimes, old hymns and national songs. It is one of the pastor's greatest sermons. It has really aroused my national feelings; I play it often.

I hope you have a very happy Christmas and blessed New Year, bleak as the outlook may be. I believe there may be a resurgence of faith and a restoration of freedom as people turn to God. God bless you all.

CHAPTER 22
Another Disappointment

20 December 1973

I was told by the major today that I would be permitted to stay in the squadron, but would have my paratrooper pay revoked. He added that I would not go on ops either as he doesn't think I am 'worth it'. What a humiliation. I will just be a piece of dead wood of use to neither man nor beast. I have the option of going to the RLI, but I think I will seek to be discharged.

24 December 1973

In the turmoil of the past several months, I have lost sight of my mission and purpose in coming to Rhodesia. My association with Baptists and missionaries made me doubt and question if what I am doing is right. I believe, however, that preaching to the African, as my friends do, is only half a Christian's responsibility.

The greatest menace to Christianity and liberty is communism and all those who share the materialistic faith that man is the supreme creative intelligence of the world. It is also my Christian duty to oppose this monster that is threatening and uprooting Christianity all over the world.

Communism, internationalism, and Zionism can only be overthrown by the power of the Gospel, the knowledge of God. The missionary strategy must be to convert the world leaders. This would end international tension, prevent nuclear destruction, and free the world of bondage. It is more important to win men of influence, for then it will be so much easier to convert the savages.

Some believe that opposing communism is getting involved in politics and that one should preach the Gospel only, without denouncing evil. But John the Baptist denounced Herod. Jesus denounced the scribes and the Pharisees. Sin and evil must be fought.

Western civilization is dying and losing to communism because it has become atheist and has lost its faith. It is the Western communists who must be opposed. Missionary work should be directed at those who now rule the West.

My purpose in coming to Rhodesia has been to fulfil my Christian duty of opposing communism in two ways. The first is to focus attention on the conspiracy by refusing to be its pawn, and by writing to expose it. The second is to actively fight communist-inspired terrorism in Africa through serving in the military. I have neglected, however, to witness for Christ and to try and win souls. This has been my great failure. I must strive to do both.

It is the failure of the missionaries that they do not preach to the most influential and articulate of our society, those who are seeking world power and who will persecute Christians if they gain that objective.

I must continue to fight communism, but ... [censored].

[The beginning of this part was also censored] ... He told me that a soldier must be very basic, and that I must come down to earth, out of orbit 'intellectually'. I have decided that I have no choice but to buy my way out of the army. The time has come.

The brigade commander, speaking at a wings parade, said that the terrorists are now applying maximum effort. There were now 200 in the country, and a further 100 on their way from training camps in Tanzania. This is crucial for Rhodesia. If success is to be had, the kill-to-contact ration must be increased, and the troops must now have the determination to win.

Also, troops must not only have pride in their regiment, but must also possess humility, for we are learning all the time and are not experts.

29 December 1973

I've submitted my article on American foreign policy to the journal *Property and Finance*. The editors are interested, and since theirs is a very conservative financial publication, they will probably print it. I am hoping the army will grant me permission.

There is a missionary group distributing copies of Reverend Richard Wurmbrand's* book, *Tortured for Christ*, to the security forces. I've circulated several copies in the SAS, and have reread it myself. Wurmbrand is so right in saying that communism will only be overthrown by the power of the Gospel. This applies to Zionism and Internationalism as well. These movements are faiths as much as they are drives for power. They are faiths that hinge on a belief that man, instead of

* A Romanian-born Christian minister of Jewish descent. After spending a second term of five years in prison for his outspoken Christian beliefs, during which time he was also tortured, he immigrated to America.

God, is the supreme being of this world. If this faith is undermined by the Gospel, then the West will be saved and the world conspirators defeated.

I am very pleased to receive the book *National Suicide: Military Aid to the Soviet Union*, by economics professor Antony C. Sutton, thank you very much. It is a very important book. Sutton has done a great service to the world by showing that the American involvement in Cold War conflicts, such as Korea and Vietnam, was only to secure multi-million dollar contracts to directly or indirectly supply war matériel to both sides of the conflict. He does not believe that America was there to fight communism.

God bless you all this New Year. It shall either be the year of salvation or the demise of our country.

31 December 1973

The eve of an onerous and threatening year that, nevertheless, may bring our salvation. It is a year that may see my change in occupation or, perhaps, my homecoming, but I would regret leaving Rhodesia. The decision will be instrumental in determining my life course and destiny.

I was put to work in the orderly room as a clerk. What a blow. Well, it will be a new experience and be helpful for me to learn organization. At least I am useful here.

1 January 1974

Once again I am wracked with uncertainty and indecision about what to do. Considering how crucial this year will be for Rhodesia, it would break me up to leave some of my best friends and mates to fight it out without me. That would be tantamount to desertion. It is true that these terrorists must be brought to know God, but in the meantime they must be stopped, whether by political or other means.

We spotted two terrs, the one with an AK, the other with an RPD machine gun.

What a routine. We get up at daybreak, then cook, eat, read, watch the enemy position three times a day, then read some more, cook again, perhaps do a quick clearance patrol, and then sleep again. The end of another 'exciting' day.

7 January 1974

Last Friday I was sent out on patrol, operating in the same area as before. This time we drove by Land Rover to the commercial farming district of Centenary, some distance north of Salisbury. This is where the first terrorist attacks occurred just over a year ago. From there we flew to Macombe basecamp on the Zambezi River in Mozambique. I'll be out for only two weeks this time, as I am actually a replacement for others who have become sick.

The Valley is now very wet, with the rain falling heavily every day. Rivers are flooding and everything is lush and green. It is quite a contrast to just a few weeks ago when everything was dry and brown. The mosquitoes are terrible now.

Last week I applied for discharge. If it is God's will for me to leave, then I'll get out. For the time being, I'm more satisfied being on operations than staying at Cranborne Barracks. I did have a very happy Christmas and New Year in Salisbury, although I missed being home. God bless you all.

13 January 1974

Going down a turbulent and unknown river and being capsized twice, is a good analogy of my army career. Should I let these two dunkings, my discharge from the officers' course and my near dismissal from the squadron, deter me from completing the five-year journey down that river? Can I accomplish more than I already have? Can I make any difference at all? I may know the answers when I return to Salisbury and HQ. Then I will learn the outcome of my request for discharge.

This op has gotten so wearisome and boring that I will be very happy to move tomorrow.

I am having trouble again mixing with my mates. I keep too much to myself and I am too quiet. An officer spoke to me about it last week, encouraging me to come out of my shell and not to be an introvert.

Sometimes I become very philosophical in my thinking. This is when I experience the most peace of mind, but I can't communicate this to the other guys as they wouldn't understand. Other times, I let myself go with the crowd, swearing, having a drink, and talking a lot of rubbish. This all in a vain attempt to be 'one of the boys', but my heart is not in it. No matter what has happened or whatever anyone has said, I feel I am as good a soldier as any, if not better.

14 January 1974

Too many missionaries here wait to be raptured away from the tribulation to which the world is doomed. Many even accept the evils of world government and Zionism as the fulfilment of Biblical prophecy. This to me is faith without works, and perhaps misguided faith at that. These people will surely be stricken by the evils they aid or refuse to resist, in spite of their teaching of the Gospel, Bible studies, and prayer meetings.

21 January 1974

I learned that the major really performed when he heard I had been out on patrol again. He shouted and screamed, "Get him back ... get him back."

So I have returned from another patrol in Mozambique. We were in the same district as before, just farther east. It was much easier this time, partly because one gets used to bush life after a while, and also because it was much cooler from the rains. The sky was constantly overcast, which helped. Water was plentiful. The Zambezi was swollen and once-dry riverbeds were flowing.

We did reconnaissance again, during which we observed a terrorist basecamp for several days. They never knew we were there, but we couldn't fire on them. Airstrikes were called in on other camps.

My patrol was withdrawn early and sent back to Salisbury to form part of a convoy to pick up the others this week. We were supposed to fly out, but the airstrips were too wet for any fixed-wing aircraft to land. Five of us therefore joined a returning RAR road convoy. What an experience that proved to be. It was normally only an eight-hour trip from the basecamp to Salisbury, but this one took us two whole days. The rains had transformed the road into a sea of mud into which our trucks sank axle-deep. We got through by sheer brute force. The trucks got stuck every 100 metres or so, when we all had to get out and push. We kept pushing through the soupy mire. The three-tonners would lumber on slowly, like huge elephants until bogging down again. The perseverance of the officers was admirable.

The performance of the black troops was a sight to behold. They would swarm around the vehicles like ants. The moment a truck was laboriously pushed out of the mud, they would spontaneously dance, shout, whistle, hug each other, or shake hands, and then run back to their vehicles with much enthusiasm. They were stripped to the waist and covered in mud.

Anyhow, I'm going to return on another convoy to fetch the others, so may be staying out for a few more weeks.

So many men have been called up that nearly every home has been affected. People are learning from their husbands, sons, and brothers how serious the situation is. The government believes that there might be a mass exodus of Europeans, and that immigration would stop if the public knew the truth. I think this will be all right, as it would leave only the hard core rooted here.

Fuel rationing begins next month. The bulk of Rhodesia's fuel comes indirectly from the Middle East, routed through South Africa.

There are big oilfields off the Angolan coast which are being opened by the Portuguese. This is promising for all of southern Africa. I may have to sell my car later as there may not be enough fuel to run it.

CHAPTER 23
Why Oppose Communism?

23 January 1974

Why am I against communism, and what is wrong with it? Communism has murdered an estimated 35 million people since the 1917 Russian Revolution. It has destroyed the souls of millions more by denying them the knowledge of Christ. It threatens Western and Christian civilization the world over.

24 January 1974

I have finished reading a book which very convincingly shows that these are the latter days prior to the second coming of Christ. But I still disagree that the Zionist capture of Palestine is a fulfilment of Biblical prophecy. The 'latter days' is one of two interpretations about the events of our time, the other being the decline and demise of Western civilization. I believe both are true, but I do not believe they are unavoidable. The trends of decay and rot can be reversed by a change of faith.

In 1926, Oswald Spengler wrote in *Decline of the West*, 'You are dying. I see in you all the characteristic stigma of decay. I can prove that your socialism, your wars and your revolutions, your atheism and your pessimism, your cynicism, your immorality, your broken-down marriages, your birth control, that is bleeding you from the bottom and killing you off at the top in your brains – can prove to you that these were characteristic marks of the dying ages of ancient states – Alexandria and Greece and neurotic Rome'.

Reverend Wurmbrand has written, "Democracy and civilization have died already in half of Europe. The rest of the world sleeps."

I believe that if faith is regained, the West and the world can be revived, and the Judgement is delayed. I think God wants this too, if I can say such a thing.

25 January 1974

There is good news to tell. I was informed today that my article in *Assegai* will be published next month in the journal *Property and Finance*. This is a great success, as this journal is circulated nationwide in business and professional circles, and in government. So not only have I told the truth to the army, but to all of Rhodesia.

Although the information may seem of more relevance to Americans, it directly affects Rhodesians. They need to know. I have been working on quite a lengthy account of the terrorist war here and the patrols on which I've been. It is something I can't publish immediately, because of government censorship, but at another time or in another country, I'm sure I could.

27 January 1974

I heard a very hard-hitting sermon that affected me for a change. The young preacher said, "God does not want our service, or good works, or deeds, and finds them nauseating unless we first give Him complete obedience." This has been my shortcoming. I have not been obedient, but with all good intentions, I have tried to work and to fight for God. It has been in the way that I think best, instead of allowing Him to work for me. God wants all of us, with nothing held back.

30 January 1974

The preacher spoke of there being body, soul, and spirit, the latter two being separate and distinct. The soul comprises the mind and personality. The spirit is the God-conscious part of us, and this is what died when man fell into sin, but it can be renewed by the Holy Ghost. The greatest threat of communism, then, is that the spirit may never be revived to God-consciousness.

31 January 1974

Last night I listened to Brother Andrew, the missionary who smuggles Bibles into communist countries. Too many Christians are affected by 'religious neutralism'. That means abstaining from the fight for their civilization and relying solely on prayer. Many others evangelize, but consider themselves above political action. They complain that their leaders and politicians are not Christians and mourn at the sad state of affairs, yet do nothing to make the Christian influence felt in their areas. Early this morning one of my mates was killed by accident. I don't know how he stood with God, but I wish I could have done more to witness to him. His loss is felt by all of us.

2 February 1974

The day before yesterday one of my mates was killed in the bush, not by terrorists, but by accident. He was shot by a member of his own patrol, who mistook him for a terr in the dark. It sounds stupid, but it can easily happen.* He was a friend of mine. I'll be part of his military funeral next week, when I'll be a member of the firing party giving a three-volley salute.

It looks as if I'll be working in the squadron office for a few weeks, where I am operating a duplicating machine. It is the first time I have done office work. I don't particularly like it, but there is much to learn here. I have an opportunity to go into the intelligence section of the squadron. If it is worthwhile, I might stay on there, but I will still take leave later this year.

Petrol rationing went into effect yesterday. There was a mad scramble by motorists to fill up the day before. I can only get about three gallons a month, which would only allow me to travel sixty miles.

Knowing the cause of the fuel shortage in the United States makes me wary of similar causes here, but I don't think the situation is exactly the same. Rhodesia, unlike America, has no oil reserves, so must import most of its fuel from South Africa. Now South Africa has also been cut back by its Middle East suppliers.

Last week Brother Andrew spoke in Salisbury. He said that persecution of Christians is more terrible than ever before because of détente with the West. Nixon and other Western leaders say nothing to criticise communist statism. This makes me sick and ashamed. Brother Andrew confirmed previous reports by Romanian Michel Sturdza and Wurmbrand. Albania, he said, is the only true communist state, as all religion has been obliterated there. The church is growing elsewhere, in spite of persecution.

Recruits for all communist armies must swear allegiance to the state and dedicate themselves to destroying its enemies. Many, he said, would, however, prefer to die rather than take the oath, but they are not allowed to die. Recall the book *Anti-Humans* [Student Re-education in Romanian Prisons] by Dumitru Bacu. He concluded that the only way to defeat the communist religion is to convert communists to Christianity.

3 February 1974

I am often told that I take myself and life too seriously. That doesn't make sense to

* Trooper Michael Morris (20) of the SAS was killed in a shooting accident in the north-eastern district of Mount Darwin, when a member of his patrol mistook him for the enemy in the dark

me. I only try to live deliberately and with purpose, not by reaction.

7 February 1974

Today my article, *The Myth of American Anti-communism*, appeared in the *Property and Finance.* God has given me the opportunity to speak the truth to all of Rhodesia. I cannot help but be proud of the heading this monthly publication wrote for me. I regret only that I could not have revised the article by adding much more to it. I have really exposed myself now; that is certain.

12 February 1974

This morning I was to parachute, but after arrival at the air base, I was not allowed. It opened my old, sore wound.

I spoke briefly to a flight sergeant, one of the para-instructors, who had heard of my article. He said I was a man after his own heart. He feels that nationalism is good for the deteriorating West, and that 'racial purity' is essential. I told him that faith in God is foremost in importance.

13 February 1974

This generation of the West must believe when there is apparently no hope; it must obey, even if it means death. It must fight to the end rather than submit. Against the spirit of heroism no material force can prevail. Nothing can defeat that except inner decadence. Destiny does not tire, nor can it be broken. Its mantle of strength descends upon those in its service.

14 February 1974

Today I was given an ultimatum to choose another corps or regiment by Monday. This is God directing my life, and I am debating what course He wants me to take. It is a good opportunity to learn engineering, medics, or signalling. Somehow I feel God wants me in the RLI. It might be best for me to start over in a new unit, although many would think me mad to go to the commandos. There is still a chance of getting a discharge.

At noon I spoke to a friend at the cathedral, who told me I am needed in the army. Is this God speaking indirectly? Do I have a mission to undertake in the RLI? The infantry is a personal challenge to me, for there I can conquer my fears and overcome my timidity. If I go back to Gwelo next year, I would only have to endure it for a year. My combat experience would help get me through the course. God must show me the way soon.

Another one of our guys was killed today: eighteen-year-old Willis,* on his first operation. I think he was a Christian, but I should have found out and encouraged him. I had accompanied him on his first jump.

16 February 1974

Another week and another man dead. This time one was killed in a contact with terrorists, the first so far. So I'll be on funeral detail next Monday.

It doesn't appear that I will be able to get a discharge from the army, but I will be leaving the SAS soon. I hope to soon be transferred to the Rhodesian Army Medical Corps (RhAMC). This will involve three months training in Bulawayo. If I succeed in that, I would still be attached to infantry units. This will be better than just basic soldiering for the rest of my time.

Enclosed is the tape by Brother Andrew, with one of the greatest messages I've ever heard, "if we do not take the Gospel to the communists, they will come to us as revolutionaries."

If you can make some recordings for me please. I would also really appreciate some tapes of the Dvořák *Slavonic Dances*, Sousa marches, Tchaikovsky's *Nutcracker Suite*, and Beethoven's *Fifth* and *Seventh Symphonies*. That would be the greatest thing you could do for me. My tape recorder has given me many hours of pleasure.

I'll just close by saying that I've had a very hard time these past few months, added to which, I have some real enemies here now. However things are going to work out all right. God is with me, so I will not regret anything I have done.

Don't get too irritated with people who often seem naïve and don't understand. It is not everyone's calling to be active in our fight.

17 February 1974

These have been difficult times for me, but I take comfort in the verse of Romans that says, 'All that happens to us is working for our good if we love God and if we are fitting into his plans'. The question is: to what end?

* Trooper Nigel Willis died from a bullet wound to the head, sustained in an ambush in Mozambique.

18 February 1974

I was part of the guard of honour for another military funeral today. I was impressed by the Gospel message of the army chaplain. Those attending have no excuse, nor can they deny that they have heard the truth of Christ being spoken to them.

20 February 1974

Today I was interviewed and accepted for a long medics' course in Bulawayo. So perhaps my hard times are over for a while. Perhaps the nausea is past. I have an excellent opportunity to become familiar with medicine … [censored].

23 February 1974

This week there has been another change of events. I am out of the SAS and into the RhAMC. I'll be doing a three-month medics' course in Bulawayo, commencing 17 April. When I finish, I'll be promoted to full corporal. This is some consolation after having been denied a commission.

After that I will be posted to some other unit, which I hope will be the RLI, based at Cranborne Barracks in Salisbury. So I'm out of the war until August. I'll be able to see the Jenkinsons again. My friend George Jenkinson received his commission last week.

In the meantime I'll be working at the army hospital in Salisbury. I'm not sure what this will entail, but it will be a new and worthwhile experience. I'll be learning something that can always be used later.

Terrorist attacks are mounting again. A farmer and a white woman were murdered near Centenary last week. Frelimo has been machine-gunning passenger trains operating between Umtali and Beira. Many Africans and whites have been killed in Mozambique as Frelimo terrorists continue to fight for control of this Portuguese territory. More and more South Africans are now coming to help us fight.

I've been seeing many Pentecostal friends as of late. They claim to speak in tongues, to be filled with the Holy Spirit, and to be really "on fire for God." However, I am still dubious. I don't think the 'performance' I saw was fraudulent, but reverence was lacking. I believe as Gamaliel, the Pharisee, "that if this work be of men it will come to nought, but if it be of God, I must not resist it."

CHAPTER 24
Zionist Opinions

2 March 1974

The fighting here is starting to increase. Patrols come back from the areas where I was, with reports of a greatly increased concentration of terrorists moving down from Tanzania and Zambia. It is no longer safe to have such small patrols. We may be losing our officer commanding since he has come down with yellow jaundice.

I heard a Zionist speak on the last Arab-Israeli war, in which he said many things of significance. A Salisbury Jew, who introduced him, declared that there is solidarity between Rhodesian Jews and Israel. He added that there is no distinction between Jew and Zionist. The speaker went on to say that the political power structure in Israel is not new, but has existed for thirty years. He claims that the United States has spent $2.2 million in aid to Israel, half the military expenditure for last year alone.

The ultimate blasphemy is that Secretary of State Henry Kissinger is so popular in Israel that he is declared 'King of the Jews'. Others are convinced that he is the antichrist.

6 March 1974

Many young people in America now believe that war is not glorious, that pollution is an urgent problem, that the American dream has not been fulfilled, and that the human race is in trouble. Their ideas have become acceptable. I, in my way, have chosen to try to help make people aware of world problems. I prefer not, however, to be used to foment a revolution by participating in leftist-socialist organizations, moratoriums, and May Day marches. These are part of the 'pressure-from-below' techniques used by communists and financed by the leftist foundations. The left wing has recognized the dehumanizing trends of industrial society, but its activism to change society has been channelled by the real revolutionaries of internationalism.

8 March 1974

I heard another Zionist speaker present some opinions contrary to the ones I heard last week. He said that the Yom Kippur War last year had serious consequences for the Israelis, as it had cost them 3,000 dead in eighteen days – men who were in the flower of their youth in a war of attrition.

In spite of United States and Israeli intelligence knowing of battle preparations at least twelve days before the Israeli army, the Arabs were able to deceive them and achieve initial military success. Even though they were taken by surprise, the Israelis still conquered more territory in the Six-Day War of 1967. But it cost them about $170 million and caused internal political upheaval.

The speaker claimed that the Shah of Iran was saying that the United States is importing more oil than ever before, and that the oil embargo is a big bluff. So what are the oil companies doing with the imports to create such shortages?

He does not believe that the Soviets will intervene directly, because too many of their troops would have to be withdrawn from Eastern Europe. These men have little battle experience, plus they are not acclimatized to the Middle East.

I'm taking advantage of my time off to consolidate in book form the notes and observations in my diary. It takes considerable concentration, but I think it will make a good testimony when finished. This is only the beginning of it. The conclusion cannot be written for years, and certainly not until the outcome of our crisis is known.

I cannot get a discharge. I must finish my last three years here, but I can still get a furlough for a couple of months. I'm just waiting to see when the best time will be to take it. Don't worry about finances for me. I can afford the trip if I sell my car. I just want to complete this medics' course and then see where I am posted.

I'm going up to Victoria Falls again next week, but that's all. I just want to get my book organised.

CHAPTER 25
My Life Mission

10 March 1974

I feel that part of my life mission is to inspire Christians to activism. This entails fighting for their Christian civilization and opposing communism, instead of just standing idly by and waiting for the end to come.

13 March 1974

The decadence of the West is not its product, but the result of its loss of contact with God.

15 March 1974

There has been a change of governing powers in France, Italy, Britain and Israel since the Yom Kippur War. The international economic situation grows more critical, with America heading for recession. This is no accident or coincidence. It has been planned that way.

17 March 1974

A friend has written to me: 'We do not fight ideas, bit people, organisations, and governments who conceal their bayonets under hypocritical slogans about human brotherhood and the rights of man'.

In the eyes of the media, the black man can do nothing wrong and the white man can do nothing right, for even his sacrifices and help are discredited. The world cares nothing for Rhodesia. Not America, Britain, or any of the sister colonies. Rhodesia is to be sacrificed. They will not help Rhodesia. It has already been written off.

There is nothing to stop Rhodesia from going all out to win its war against terrorism, but the government is scared of criticism. Rhodesian allows Harry Oppenheimer's Anglo-American Corporation to influence Rhodesian security. While Zambia harbours terrorists, Rhodesia's best sanction against her would be to cut off her supply of electricity from Kariba. But this action is not taken because the Anglo-American copper mines and smelters in Zambia would shut down as a result.

Rhodesia does not take Zambian President Kenneth Kaunda's declaration of war or the Chinese influence in Zambia seriously. Rhodesia is too scared of world opinion to do anything, but world opinion is nothing more than propaganda. The British press claims that Rhodesia has increased trade with Red China by two-thirds. Rhodesia does not use its strategic chrome as a weapon of boycott against other nations. Rhodesia has nothing to lose by this. It has only its survival to gain.

19 March 1974

What are my reasons for being a Christian and accepting Christ as my Saviour?

1. the reality and rationality of the universe. Although science may not prove God, it points towards His existence – the laws of thermodynamics and entropy, and the conservation of energy. The universe is too complicated to have happened by chance or accident. There is the biological law that all life comes from pre-existing life. All other theories remain unproven, and also accepted by faith.
2. there is the spiritual nature of man, his personality, and his emotions.

20 March 1974

One of the shortcomings of many patriotic groups is their lack of a spiritual basis. God's role is forgotten or rejected, yet this is the only source of strength that will give us victory. We will not win on economic, political, racial, materialistic, or capitalistic grounds. The political climate of 1776 will never return as too much of the American spirit is lost. Western civilization can only be salvaged if we return to its basis of Christianity.

I've been working hard writing a testimony that I hope will contribute towards this. It is too short really to be a book, but I'll add to it as the outcome of the great crisis unfolds. I know a man who can publish it, but the problem will be trying to sell it. I've also written an article for a Baptist publication to try to motivate them to take an interest and participation in world problems, instead of waiting for the Second Coming. That one will appear at Easter. [This is the article 'Christian Activism' of Chapter 1].

It was a great day at Victoria Falls last Saturday. From the air it is really spectacular to see it in flood. I travelled up the Zambezi on a pontoon for tourists, where I met people from Missouri and Switzerland. I witnessed to the Swiss chap, and the Missouri missionaries took it from there. Along the way we saw herds of Cape buffalo and zebra.

My hairline is receding now. I suppose it's from worrying too much, but I'm still happy. Today marks the beginning of my third year here and the end is not in sight. I still intend to go on leave, but this depends on me being able to sell my story.

It is good to hear that my former Sunday school pupils are doing well.

27 March 1974

I've returned to work in the hospital storeroom at KGVI Barracks. It is one of the easiest jobs in the army. I don't really like it, but I enjoy the people there.

The basic problem is that I want to be free. I want to be an independent man, not an organization man, and there is nothing more organised than the army. Yet I had to join. By submitting myself to this organization I can oppose the controlled 'American Establishment' that would create a world socialist organization to enslave us all.

My inability to completely submit to organization has caused me much grief and embarrassment because, sometimes, I think too much for myself, instead of having confidence in those in authority over me.

I have made mistakes which have been my own fault. I cannot blame it on bad luck or circumstances. I hope I can somehow redeem myself before leaving the army.

It appears that, just as America has been sending aid to communist countries during the Vietnam War, so Rhodesia is extending a helping hand to Zambia even though it harbours terrorists. I refused to serve in the American forces because of this treachery. Now I must face it here.

31 March 1974

When I lived in America I was in contact with some of the conservatively-oriented, patriotic organizations which express varying degrees of concern for the state of the republic, ranging from mere discussion to militancy. Some try to educate an apathetic public, while others watch for every bill or amendment before Congress that might be detrimental to America, or that would undermine the American constitution. Others form units and semi-military resistance to oppose any foreign or domestic tyranny that might threaten American freedom and independence. Others still attempt to organize a counter-revolutionary force against the militant left and the divergent minority groups controlled by it.

The basis of race, culture, and nation is vital for the survival of Western civilization. Blood and soil, conservation and nationalism, are what make a country and civilization sound, strong, and healthy.

But faith is needed. Faith in our way of life, our civilization, in a higher destiny and the divine sanction of God – that He is using us to work good in His creation.

I believe that the actions of these groups are necessary, but they need a spiritual basis for victory. Our civilization is still a contest of faiths. But faith in nation, race, or free enterprise, not backed by faith in God, will never match the faith of communism.

The enemies of our freedom and civilization will not be effectively opposed on an economic or political basis alone. A spiritual basis is needed.

7 April 1974

A pastor prayed today for "peace in our time", but never, never do they pray for victory. Most people are convinced that they cannot win this war, a belief which is in itself a psychological victory for the communists.

Rhodesians must have faith in themselves, in their country, and in the belief that God is on their side. There will never be peace until our enemies are defeated and we have victory. We will never have peace by appeasement or compromise. Communists and revolutionaries are on our doorstep. There will never be peace until they are destroyed or defeated, or their hearts are changed by conversion.

Rhodesia is undergoing a war of psycho-politics. The people are being made to believe that they cannot win, but Rhodesia could be the Thermopylae of southern Africa.

8 April 1974

I believe in God and Jesus Christ by faith. Although there is much evidence to indicate the fact of God's existence and his creation of the universe, neither I nor anyone else can absolutely prove it. There is no way around it – confession of God's existence is an act of faith.

10 April 1974

Last night I spoke to a Christian man who is convinced that he must never resort to violence to defend himself, or fight in any way, even for his life and liberty. He feels that communism should not be opposed by arms, and that the second coming of Christ will occur before the communists could take over the world. He believes that all governments, no matter how evil or corrupt, are ordained by God. For this man, Christianity has destroyed his instinct for survival and his will to resist evil. If every Christian were to think this, we would be doomed.

14 April 1974

Today is the resurrection day of our Lord; the day that not only marked victory over death and hell, but also assured victory for those who worship and serve Him.

I've gone to Bulawayo where I am staying with a policeman and his family. Although not religious, they have common sense and a strong instinct for survival and the welfare of their country.

I met a couple who fled from Mobuto's persecution in the Congo. They lost all their property and their business was seized. This is a living lesson for those who want communist rule.

15 April 1974

I again visited with the people who fled the Congo. The woman was kept in a prison under deplorable conditions. After having all their property confiscated, they came to Rhodesia, where they arrived with nothing except their jeep. As they travelled through Zambia, they saw many Chinese accompanying units of the Zambian army.

Today I moved into Llewellin Barracks, the biggest military camp in Rhodesia. All the national servicemen who have to serve for one year are trained here. I share a room with a good friend of mine from the SAS. Conditions are quite decent. We are in the heart of Matabeleland, about ten miles from Bulawayo. The old hunting grounds of the Matabele, it is grassland and quite beautiful, much like the Great Plains back home.

I've been going out with a girl from Hamilton, Ohio, whom I met last November.

CHAPTER 26
Medics' Training

20 April 1974

[The journal was censored from 20 April to 26 June 1974. This space is therefore filled in with letters written home, together with a supplement written during the medics training exercise in June of that year.]

I started the medics' course this week, and so far it is really difficult, with much to learn in a short space of time. It is a burden for me, because I want to do well, so that I can make something useful of myself in the army. If I don't make it, I'll leave the country. It is God's will whether I stay or not, because I am doing my best.

29 April 1974

The first phase of the medics' course on anatomy has been completed, for which I did well in the exams. This week we begin on physiology. Each of us will work one day a week in the camp hospital, treating patients and learning hospital procedure. This is the training depot for all draftees. Some fake sickness or injury to try to get out of doing their national service. There are whites, Africans, and Coloureds here, plus an occasional Chinese.* One doesn't appreciate the quality of character you get in the SAS until you see this bunch.

I would like to study the book *Psycho-Chemical Warfare.*

4 May 1974

Rhodesian air force planes have been shot down during the past few weeks.† All the news media say that they had crashed, but the terrs are being supplied with the portable SAM heat-seeking missile. About the only thing a pilot can do if one of these is fired at him, is to fly directly into the sun, then cut away at a sharp angle. It works … sometimes.

* At this stage of the war, black Africans were not subjected to national conscription. If they wished to serve, they could volunteer for one of the regular units such as the all-black, white-officered RAR. It was only right at the end of the war that blacks were conscripted, but only those with certain laid-down minimum educational qualifications.

† On 14 April, an air force Aermacchi AL-60 'Trojan' was shot down by anti-aircraft fire north of Cahora Basa Dam in Mozambique, killing both crew members. Six days later, another Trojan, sent to search for the one that was missing, was brought down with a SAM-7 ground-to-air missile. Both on board died. The Trojans were not combat aircraft, but single-propeller aircraft primarily used for reconnaissance.

The work on the course has eased now, making it very interesting and enjoyable. We even have a good time. Soon I'll have to choose where to be posted, but I hope to go back to the squadron so that I can carry on parachuting. I could go anywhere – Inyanga, Kariba, Wankie, or even the very arid south-western border area of Matabeleland.

I want to wish you a happy Mother's Day, Mom. I love you and appreciate the understanding and support you've given me while I've been away. I still don't regret coming here, in spite of some of the difficulties I've had. I still think it is worthwhile, and I have much hope for this country.

12 May 1974

Many thanks for sending me the book *The Suicide of Europe*, by Prince Sturdza. It will be well worth reading again.

I came across a passage by a former Archbishop of Canterbury, which I think most Christians would do well to heed:

> Let us at all costs avoid the temptation to make our Christian worship a withdrawal from the stress and sorrow of life into a realm of unreal beauty. It was the real world that Christ came into, a city where there was no room for him, and into a country where Herod, the murderer of innocents, was king.
>
> He comes to us, not to shield us from the harshness of the world, but to give us the courage and strength to bear it, not to snatch us away by some miracle from the conflict of life, but to give us peace, His peace in our hearts, by which we may be calmly steadfast while the conflict rages, and be able to bring to the world that healing that is peace.

If I don't take my leave now, I could finish my enlistment six months early in 1975, rather than in March 1977. I am about halfway through at this point.

Yesterday I passed a fitness test. Devised by some health organization, everyone in the army must try to pass it at some time. I won a gold medal, which will maintain the excellent public image of the SAS, something, however, I don't think it really deserves. The hardest part was to pay $2.75 for the medal. I had to run three miles, do various exercises, and swim 300 yards.

Next week we begin working in the Mpilo African hospital in Bulawayo, where we will learn stitching and treatments. It should be good training.

Portugal is developing a new role for itself in Africa, making me apprehensive about what could happen. New Portuguese head of state, General António de Spínola, [following the military assuming power during the so-called Carnation Revolution] is going to let Frelimo become a legitimate political party in Mozambique, without it having to give up its arms.

18 May 1974

There was good news for me this week. My story of the counter-insurgency patrol will be published in the June issue of *Assegai*.

I am still not sure of what is happening in Portugal. De Spinola claims Portuguese forces will remain in Africa. It is very important for Rhodesia that they do, as we could never bear the brunt of a full-scale guerrilla war. We must have help from Portugal and South Africa. We especially need South Africa, as that nation's actions will decide the future of southern Africa. With the full military support of South Africa, Rhodesia could win quickly through military operations.

It is not comforting to hear that de Spinola has been releasing prisoners and communists from jails, or that there is a resurgence of the Communist Party and labour unions in Portugal.

The army has offered to pay my way through the School of Medicine at the University of Rhodesia. I have the qualifications, so I am tempted to try. I am, however, reluctant to return to school for another six years. I'm not sure what to do, but I've applied for acceptance.

My course is going well. We are currently doing practical field first aid, and studying diseases. I am glad the time is going fast. I don't like the barracks so I'll be glad to get away.

I am now an instructor for my course. I do it as we did at Quantico – the Marine way. The army has abandoned the Macombe basecamp on the Zambezi in Mozambique where we worked last year. This is very bad news. The whole area of Mozambique that we patrolled is now overrun with Frelimo. In other words, we and the Portuguese have lost that area. All that sweat, dirt, and heat for a delaying action only. We have captured enough AK47 assault rifles and ammunition to use if need be in place of our own weapons.

25 May 1974

It looks as if the communists are getting a hold on the Portuguese government. There is fear that Mozambique may become another Congo, although the new military junta in Lisbon claims it will not pull out its forces. In Beira and Lourenço Marques there have been racially- motivated incidents of violence and rioting, precipitated by Frelimo, now recognized as a legitimate political party. The South Africans are fortifying their border with Mozambique.

Thanks for the article on the Bilderberg meeting.* No doubt it is connected with this year's turnover in the leadership of so many countries.

I drove out to the Matopos as I promised my batman that I would take him to his kraal on Saturday. It is very interesting to see how these people live away from white influence. The Matabele [correctly amaNdebele] are a proud race, very hospitable and likeable. Their simple agricultural lifestyle isn't bad at all, and the countryside is beautiful.

8 June 1974

After I finish the course on 12 July, I'm being posted back to the RLI battalion based in Salisbury. I'll be spending a considerable amount of time in the Rhodesian operational areas. I like Salisbury the best, but I also like the bush life, as long as we don't stay for too long.

I was not given a discharge as I decided not to leave. I wanted to leave earlier when I was so disappointed and everything seemed to be going wrong. Things are going very well now, and I have some excellent opportunities for advancement. I feel that I can do more and be more effective against communism and the internationalists by staying in the army.

Not only can I have the opportunity to actively oppose the advance of communism in Africa militarily, but also write about it so as to inform people of the worldwide conspiracy confronting us. I could not have written any of my articles if I had not come here.

People will listen to you if you arouse their interest by dramatic action.

The crucial stage is now upon us, particularly since Mozambique may soon be

* An annual conference designed to enhance interaction between Europe and North America. Every year, more than 100 political leaders and experts from national spheres of finance, economics and industry, as well as academics and the media, are invited to take part in the conference

lost. A friend pointed out to me the parallels between the de Spinola government and the 1917 Russian provisional government of Alexander Kerensky, a transition to a communist takeover. Hopefully Portugal will have a counter movement as in Chile. In order to be lenient and 'progressive', de Spinola, like Kerensky, released from detention all the subversives, communists and radicals.

In spite of the liberal tendencies of the Smith government toward settlement policies which will lead to majority rule, the crisis at hand will clarify the white position here, as the Europeans watch a repeat of events in the Congo taking place in next door Mozambique.

I am going to make my stand here. I want to stay.

This week I'll be taking a twelve-man patrol out on a two-week exercise in the Matopos, as part of our practical field work.

A friend of mine was killed a few days ago when he was blown up by a mine that took part of his leg off. He later died of his wounds, apparently as a result of fat from the bloodstream depositing in his lungs. His name was Ken Smith, one of the best soldiers we had.*

There has been an outbreak of German measles in the camp, resulting in the hospital filling up. I have avoided the disease so far, in spite of treating the patients.

28 June 1974

[A letter home from John]

I just returned from our two-week field exercise in the Matopos where we had quite a time.

While on the exercise, our chief instructor, Mr Strauss, told me that someone from the School of Infantry had tried to prevent me from getting on the medics' course, but he wouldn't have it.

Anyhow, I want to stick it out here for a while more to see if I can get into medical school at the university. Also, Mr Strauss is trying to form a special unit of para-medics to jump into places where there would otherwise be no medical assistance. I would like to do that. There would be plenty of action, but in a non-combatant

* Lance Corporal Kenneth Richard Smith of the SAS died as a result of an anti-personnel mine explosion. Having lost a leg at the time of the explosion, which occurred during an external operation near Chimoio, Mozambique, Ken died in Salisbury Central Hospital from a fatty embolism in the blood stream. He was an Australian national who had formerly served with the Australian SAS.

role, for which I am more suited. I just want to wait first and see what happens.

I ended up as section commander on the exercise. I was placed in charge of nine men, which I thoroughly enjoyed. We did plenty of practical first aid, including giving intravenous infusions while under battle conditions. We were set up in a non-tactical basecamp where we could have cooking fires and therefore fresh, cooked food.

We did some marching around the hills, adding to a very enjoyable two weeks. It gets very cold at night, with frost sometimes, but the days are warm and sunny.

My article on the counter-insurgency patrol has been published in the latest issue of *Assegai*. I received four dollars for it. It was, however, disappointing to see the alterations and revisions made. The entire section on the communist threat to southern Africa and the strategic importance of Rhodesia has been deleted. My comments on the morale of the forces were transformed into propaganda for the SAS. I'm therefore not going to try to get it published in other magazines. I want to tell things the way they are.

Probably the paper you had sent to my friends was too 'extreme' for them. They are nice people but, like most nice people, they cannot bear to hear the truth being spoken. I've seen these folk twice since being here, and will visit them again before returning to Salisbury. Their son and I are still good friends, but our separate careers, since last year, have put us in two different worlds of the army, so I don't see him much.

I'm glad this course is nearly over; I'll be pleased to return to Salisbury again, even to the operational areas, as I can then continue with my writing. The RLI will be a new experience also.

8 July 1974

Since 1972, when the United States army morale and fighting spirit were broken by the Vietnam conflagration, heroin addiction, racial conflict, and the collapse of discipline, there has been an attempt to rebuild the army. At first the army tried pampering and the permissive country-club approach, but this demoralized the army even more. When General Creighton Abrams returned from Vietnam to become army chief of staff, he toughened training and restored discipline for on-duty hours. In order to reinstitute professionalism, the army initiated an all-volunteer force.

Professionalism is essential for an efficient and well-trained army, but the greatest damage caused by Vietnam remains – the loss of purpose. The army may become a force like ancient Rome's Praetorian Guard, dedicated to nothing but itself and professionalism, a mercenary force selling its military power to political forces. Nationalism, dedication to country, protection of freedom, and security of interests at home and overseas, have yet to be re-instilled.

Since the overthrow of the Caetano regime in Portugal, Rhodesia and South Africa may have to stand guard alone over their civilization in southern Africa. Although the overseas Portuguese territories of Angola, Mozambique and Portuguese Guinea are essential for the survival of Portugal, the new leftist-oriented government of de Spinola may cause their eventual abandonment to African communists.

The new government has attempted settlement with Frelimo in Mozambique, although military operations continue. Frelimo is closer than ever to achieving a capitulation from a war-weary country. White inhabitants are alarmed at the prospect of black rule, and are organizing resistance. Very probably, they will be betrayed by a government seeking political solutions. The question is, why?

Evidence of a swing to the left can be seen in the introduction of socialists and communists into the new government in Portugal, like Mário Soares and Álvaro Cunhal. There has also been a release from prisons of leftist activists. This could be the communist takeover of Portugal, or it may be a ... [The journals were censored from 8 July to 3 November 1974. This period is filled in with letters written home.]

10 July 1974

I finished my medics' course last Friday. With an average score of eighty-three percent, I was placed fifth in the class. I am now a full corporal and a qualified medic. At least now I will be getting an extra fifty dollars a month, which will help.

As I've told you, I've been posted to the a commando battalion, the RLI. This means, that as soon as I am transferred and settled in, I will be going back to the north-east war zone [Operation *Hurricane*]. I'm looking forward to it, as I have not been out of here since January. It will be a great experience to see a counter-insurgency war first hand. As for Portugal, I would add that the coup is an attempt by the internationalist-controlled oil companies to grab the oil in Angola.

There is an early election coming up here. Ian Smith and his Rhodesian Front Party are losing confidence, but they want to stay in power. He came on national radio and gave a very reassuring and conservative-sounding address.* The atmosphere, however, is tense and fearful, and many people are leaving the country.

* The elections were held on 30 July; the Rhodesian Front took all fifty white seats.

CHAPTER 27
Back to the RLI

27 July 1974

Sorry not to have written for a while, but I've been restricted to camp and have not been able to get postage stamps. Sometimes I have to work weekends – not busy work, but we just have to be there.

I like what I am doing now. It is interesting, added to which I have responsibilities and a good bunch to work with. I will be leaving for the operational area soon, which makes me glad as this is where everything is happening. It is where I will get my medical experience.

I believe I am fulfilling God's will for my life. Even though some of us may contribute little or nothing to our culture, there are those who are called on to keep our civilization alive. That burden is mine, but sometimes I also drift into my own little world, away from reality, where I become like a cork floating on the tide. Events seem so overwhelming at times. Then I pray for guidance and understanding.

Terrorism is spreading to the city. A grenade was thrown into a nightclub frequented by soldiers, injuring several people. Police say they do not know who is responsible.

To isolate the terrs, thousands of tribesmen are being resettled in protected villages. The programme, along with the government offering cash rewards to informers, has been successful.

I was glad to meet up with another American. He comes from North Carolina, and enlisted this week. He was a Marine with the Sixth Fleet in the Mediterranean.

I helped the officer commanding the SAS, Major Robinson* prepare a paper on *Leadership Under Operational Conditions*, which he wanted for his staff course. I provided him with ideas for it, drawing from my own experience of success and failure, and from personal observations I have made since being in the army. Some points were slams against him, because, although he means well, his discipline

* Later Lieutenant-Colonel Brian G. Robinson OLM, MCM. As a major he commanded the squadron since January 1973. He was appointed an Officer of the Legion of Merit (OLM) for consistently proving himself to be an exceptional field commander who spared no effort to ensure the safety of his troops and the success of his missions, and for rendering distinguished service to Rhodesia over and above the normal call of duty.

policies have done more to lower morale in the squadron than those of anyone I have ever seen.

The Portuguese situation continues to deteriorate as army units in Mozambique refuse to carry on fighting. Last week one unit even defected to the other side. We hear some proclaiming that Frelimo is the only representative political force in that country.

The prospects of getting home soon on leave seem bleak now. My pay increase has not come through yet. I hope to pay off my car with that.

Well, at any rate, I'm content and enjoying life. A medic lives in anticipation of the 'big moment' when he has to handle an emergency, and lives are in his hands. I just hope I can handle my big moment when it comes. It must.

Keep fighting and do not be discouraged by seeming defeat.

17 August 1974

For the past two weeks, I've been out of town covering a training exercise of the RLI recruits at a national park near Que Que. I haven't been to the operational areas since January, nor have I been on patrol since then.

It looks as though Mozambique is lost. What happened to the United States army in Vietnam has now happened to the Portuguese army – a complete collapse of morale and the will to fight.

Frelimo, for the time being, seems content with Mozambique. And now the other terrorist organizations, the military wings of ZANU and ZAPU, ZANLA and ZIPRA respectively, are operating in Rhodesia. We've had success against them recently, killing off two big gangs and their leaders, who had caused us much trouble this past year.

One of our majors was killed last week* and, in a separate incident, a helicopter shot down. There has been no escalation of fighting because of the Mozambique situation. Frelimo claims it is only interested in 'liberating' Portuguese East Africa. There is an article in a South African news magazine about a certain KGB agent who had been working in Mozambique at the time of the coup. One of many, I suppose. I cannot predict how things will turn out here. Most white Rhodesian families have been in Rhodesia for several generations and so have nowhere else they can call home.

* Major Ernest 'Doomps Addams of HQ, 2 Brigade, was killed by a terrorist hiding in a tree.

They will stay and fight, I'm pleased to say. They understand their position racially and historically, but come short politically.

Ian Smith's party, the Rhodesian Front, won the election overwhelmingly, which is good if it sticks to party principles and promises. I fully anticipate compromise and political 'solutions', unless the white citizens can stop it. I still have more hope for Rhodesia than for any other country. A friend of mine feels that the only way the United States can survive as a world power is to control its confused and directionless ethnic fragmentation. He does not mean a dictatorship of internationalists or CFR. He feels that the days of the Republic are over, and that we must try to restore some of the lost freedom and opportunity.

I don't always go to church now because I can't find one in which I get anything out of the service, although there is a good one in Bulawayo that I liked.

I have a range of 'acquaintances' here, from missionaries to revolutionaries. I wouldn't call them all 'friends' but somehow, I've come to mix with them. I've dated the girl from Hamilton, Ohio, a few times since I met her last November. She is a Baptist missionary. Most of the Americans I've met here are missionaries. Many seem liberal too, which does not put them in good standing with the government. Some have said the wrong things concerning the African's position here.

I met a fellow from Minnesota who has joined the RLI because he feels the battle for our civilization is more clear-cut and active here.

As you can imagine, my everyday life is dominated by the soldiers with whom I spend all my time working, playing, eating, and living. It is not always easy, but I get along okay with them. I'm proud to be a part of this army. It's been a grand experience.

If I go to medical school, it will be in 1976, as I applied too late to get into the University of Rhodesia next year.

Happy birthday, Dad. Next year you will be at the half century mark, and I'll be at the quarter century. I don't know if there is any significance in that. Thanks for being a great dad.

24 August 1974

This may be the last letter I can write for a few weeks, since I'm going out to the border again. Working with the commando battalion will be a new experience for me, and I'm glad I can go. It will be good to get away from Salisbury, to see more action, and to further my medical experience. With new experiences to write about, I can increase my journalistic endeavours.

The struggle for Western civilization is most clear-cut and apparent here. Unfortunately, Rhodesia is doing a fine job of fighting terrorism and communism on the enemy's terms. Although we are on the defensive, Rhodesians have not been hit hard enough to have their fighting spirit really aroused. Most white people are still secure in their cities and on their farms, well away from the operational areas. I believe that will change. I'll be here to see how it turns out in the next few of years.

I lost another friend of mine this week, Cpl Gary Lloyd, who did the medics course with me in Bulawayo. He had been on my patrol in the Matopos, a really good guy, and only eighteen years old. He was blown up by a landmine.*

Two days ago I did a lumbar puncture on one of the RLI troopers at Salisbury Central Hospital in town. I was quite pleased that the doctor had the confidence to let me do it. It is a simple operation, once you know how. The nurses are quite jealous because army medics are allowed to do many things that they are not. Some of them watched while I did it.

5 September 1974

I have gone out on operations again, but things are completely different from my patrols with the SAS. Positioned in a basecamp several miles from Mount Darwin in the northeast of Rhodesia, I am able to write, to receive mail, and to have many of the comforts of home, such as eating from a table, taking a shower, sleeping on a cot, and listening to the radio. The greatest danger is from the numerous landmines planted on nearby roads. Some are detonated every day. Occasionally I make the trip to the little town of Mount Darwin, accompanying the resupply convoys, which are hot, dusty, and miserable. But it is part of my job, as a medic, to go.

Most of the time I sit in this abandoned mission, waiting for casualties to come in, or treating minor aches, pains, and complaints. One captured terr was brought in with a gunshot wound in his leg, which we treated while he was being interrogated. One of the mechanics was burned badly while cleaning an engine. I like the work, but would prefer to be in more of a combatant role.

* A territorial, Corporal Gary James Lloyd of 3 (Independent) Company, the Rhodesia Regiment, was killed by a landmine on the Bveke-Mukumbura loop road, Mt Darwin, on 22 August 1974.

We are really on the frontier of Western civilization in places like this, the front line and outer periphery. That is very apparent once you leave a metropolitan area like Salisbury. The contrast between the African and European way of life is manifest in this raw, rugged environment. The towns of Mount Darwin, Centenary, and Bindura are all garrisoned, and are the jumping-off points for operations. They are agricultural centres, and the only after-hours activity available is the pub. The camps and barracks are made of earth and corrugated iron, in much the same style as the forts of the Old West.

Operations have been successful, but the cost has run up the national deficit into millions of dollars, paid by the 250,000 white people of this country. A ten percent income tax surcharge has been introduced to try and bring it down.

Mozambique is being handed over to Frelimo by the Portuguese. Now Rhodesia will soon bear the full brunt of the communist advance on southern Africa.

Rhodesia has a new national anthem. It is to the music of *Ode to Joy* from the fourth movement of Beethoven's Ninth Symphony, my favourite symphony. I'm glad that I've come to Rhodesia, and to have been able to see and to live such an experience. Sometimes I wonder if I will ever be able to go home. Somehow, at this point it seems doubtful. It is not an easy life, but at least it is eventful and significant historically. That is what is important to me.

20 September 1974

Today marks the midpoint of my five-year enlistment. I've completed thirty months and have thirty more to go. This last week of the current operation has been an eventful one for me. Nothing had happened the first three weeks, and I was so bored just sitting at basecamp. I went to the commanding officer and requested to go out with the troops, not only as a medic, but also as an infantryman.

Over the next four days I participated in four helicopter-borne assaults on terrorists who had crossed over the border, but only on two of them was there any fighting. I had my first battle casualties to treat. On the first assault we drove the terrs out of a kraal complex, going through in extended line, using mass firepower and calling on helicopter gunships and air strikes for support. One of the enemy had fled just before we attacked, and we thought another was hit. I fell out of line to fix up some African casualties and had them casevaced to Salisbury. I spent the night there before flying back to our base.

We had no military casualties that day, but on the next one we were not so fortunate. Going out again on the airborne assault, we landed and formed up on an extended line of attack. We were fired on while crossing a wooden fence, and one of my mates, Philip Lord from Kenya, was hit about twenty yards from me. After returning fire, the others continued the assault and succeeded in killing ten terrorists. I tried to save Lord by cardiac massage and artificial respiration. He had internal damage and bleeding. Being in such deep shock, though, he died in the helicopter on the returning casevac.*

Fortunately for him, he was unconscious the whole time. Strangely enough, he knew before he left that he would die, and he commented that he would not come back alive. Yet he volunteered to go in the place of another trooper. It seems in some cases, we are forewarned of death and can prepare ourselves for it, as this soldier did.

At least we have had success, if not a victory, and this op was worthwhile for my unit. I've seen more action this week than in my entire previous service. I love it, and wouldn't have it any other way now.

I've done something unconventional for medics. Usually they don't accompany the assault and attack forces at all, let alone go onto the front lines as I was doing. I feel that I should be there if any of our guys get hit. I love these men because they are brave and are not afraid to die. I've gained the confidence and respect of this unit, because I went in with them when I could have stayed in camp.

Even though I do not entirely agree with this government's way of fighting the war, I feel a loyalty to the unit and men with whom I serve. An overpowering spirit and feeling grips you when you go on the attack. There is the desire and drive to meet the enemy and destroy him. It is the moment, so brief and fleeting, for which you train and endure. It is your purpose for being a soldier, the reason for your existence. This has been an answer to prayer, because the former boredom was maddening, and this is the best way to live.

I'll be having two weeks' leave in Salisbury in a few days, but will then return. It is important to me to remain a combat soldier and a specialist medic, because only then will some people listen to you when you attempt to explain the bigger issues.

* Lance corporal Charles Philip Lord (24), of Support Group, 1st Battalion, the Rhodesian Light Infantry, died from gunshot wounds sustained in a contact in the Kandeya TTL, Mount Darwin.

The battle for Rhodesia is only one such issue.

I've learned a great deal in this operation, but I'm not exposing myself to any unnecessary risks. I'm going where I should be to do my job. This is a school ground for military experience, and the infantry unit I'm posted to now is really the shock troop of this army. I wouldn't be anywhere else just now. I know you will understand that. It is a chance to use what leadership I have, and it has boosted the morale of my fellow soldiers.

Happy anniversary, Mom and Dad. God bless.

29 September 1974

I've come back to town for two weeks, but will be going back to the 'sharp end' again for a month. I work with the Support Group commando of RLI that specializes in mortars, tracking, and manning armoured cars. I enjoy working with them, and even find it preferable to the SAS, although I do miss the parachuting.

Someone has advised me not to tell you too much of what I'm doing because it will make you worry. I think you would prefer to know. Unlike the other medics who usually stay behind when the troops go out, I go with my guys and serve as both medic and infantryman. So on helicopter assaults I am in the line of attack with my men when someone gets hit. I prefer this combatant role to the boredom of sitting in basecamp. It also boosts the morale and confidence of the troops to have their medic with them, right there on the spot when things get hot. They respect me for it too.

The lead article of this month's *Property and Finance* is a tremendous exposé of the internationalist conspiracy. The editor has references and quotes from my own article concerning the CFR.

I now feel that I am accomplishing what I joined the army for: to help stop, militarily, the spread of communism on the ground, and to make people aware of the conspiratorial forces behind it.

On my days off before my next tour of duty, I am writing a new story based on recent experiences. I am getting good medical practice treating gunshot wounds and war injuries. Since my return, I've performed another lumbar puncture at the city hospital.

Thanks very much for the book *Psycho-Chemical Warfare*, which I'm reading now.

13 October 1974

I have returned again to the operational areas. I'll be spending most of my time here now, until I either leave or start medical school, if that works out. I'm quite happy being here, as long as I'm in an active role. I go on patrol or on helicopter assaults when we are acting as 'Fireforce', at Mount Darwin.* This is where I can accomplish my objective of participating in counter-insurgency war, destroying guerrilla forces, giving medical treatment to the wounded, and being there to make an effective Christian witness to the men.

I will have paid off my car in four months. I will then be able to start saving, and hope that I'll have enough to come home in a year's time, if conditions permit. I have become so thoroughly enmeshed in events in this part of the world, that I want to stay to see the outcome. I feel that I have found my historical role here and, once that is finished, I don't know what I will do.

In the meantime, I hope to participate in an endurance exercise next month in the Eastern Highlands. This is the mountain district of Rhodesia, my favourite area.

It has pleased me that I've been able to meet and to get along with such a variety of people. Those who impress me the most are the Rhodesian farmers who, as police reservists, spend two to three months a year patrolling, ambushing, and fighting terrorism. They remind me of [the Roman aristocrat and farmer] Cincinnatus, and you won't find many countries where a farmer will put down the plough to pick up a gun like our American frontiersmen once did.

* The Fireforce concept of vertical envelopment of the enemy has its origins in the Rhodesian bush war of the 1970s. First employed by the SAS in Mozambique in 1973, Fireforce quickly evolved into a highly effective rapid-reaction response to a reported terrorist position. On twenty-four hour standby, and based at one of the forward bases such as Mount Darwin, would be elements from one of Rhodesia's regular units such as the RLI or RAR. Four-man sticks would be flown out in Alouette III helicopters called G-Cars. Such a flight would be accompanied by a K-Car Alouette, armed with a 20mm cannon, and which was the aerial platform for the commander to coordinate the engagement with his troops on the ground. Where there were larger groups of insurgents sighted, Dakota-borne paratroopers would also be dropped at very low level.

CHAPTER 28
Finding My Place: Fireforce Medic

27 October 1974

I am still in the bush and have another week before going back to town. This has been a very bad trip so far, as I've been sitting in basecamp the whole time. It is unbearable sitting in one place doing nothing, even though we are right in the middle of the so-called war zone. HQ is not for me. If all goes well, this will be the last time I have to do this. I went to the commanding officer of the battalion and asked him for a different posting, specifically to Mount Darwin where I can join the assault troops as a permanent Fireforce medic. This is what I was doing last time out. It is the only position in this army with which I have been truly and completely satisfied, and it has taken me this long to find it. I don't want to lose it now. I guess I am more of an infantryman than a medic, and I'm only happy when I'm where the action is.

I find that when one tries to motivate and to activate complacent people to wake up from their own little worlds, and to start fighting for their country, civilization, and way of life, they will not listen to you unless you have committed yourself fully to the effort and they can see your example. This is why I asked for this new posting.

I have an inner peace because I trust God to look after my safety and, even if I do get drilled [shot] one day, I'll have the inner satisfaction of knowing that I achieved my purpose in this country, and that I gave all that I could. It is most important to do that, even though others may betray you. It is the only way I can give an effective Christian witness, not with words, but by a life committed to what I consider to be my responsibility as a man and a Christian – my historical mission in life.

I am so fully involved in this now, that I sometimes wonder just what I would do if this world were peaceful and not in crisis.

Thanks very much for sending the two books by Hendrik van der Breggen. I believe his method of dealing with the problem of religious neutralism is tremendous, and it has helped me to deal with it also.

I've met some very remarkable people on the frontier. There is a Mr Rose with us, who is the son of one of the original pioneers in the area. He has lived and worked in this region for over forty years. He is sixty-two, but still serves on patrols as a tracker with the army, and he can outwalk any of the younger guys. The outdoor life has kept him in the peak of fitness. He is also wanted by the terrorists and has a price on his head. There are few places where you can find such men.

3 November 1974

At long last this bush trip is drawing to a close and, although it has been a disappointment in some ways, in others it has been very significant as I've learned much. Militarily, I've accomplished nothing, for I've hardly been out of HQ. However, I've been able to witness for my faith, primarily in my memorial service for Stockhill a week ago. The Support Group knows I am a Christian.

I have been able to help several of the chaps with their emotional problems, when they were in need of someone to talk to and to help them bear their burdens. I've made one new friend and another old friend understands me and my motivations, and that has been a help.

Medically, I feel more confident and experienced, although I've had no serious injuries to treat. I don't feel that I've improved my standard, but I have maintained it. When I return to Mount Darwin next week, I hope to fulfil my mission here, by going out on Fireforce into the heat of fighting and action, whatever there is of it. I pray for success in this. If I do not find action soon, I shall be lost. It is evident to me now just how low the morale of Support Group is, and what I could have and should have done to help boost it. It is my duty as an NCO and professional soldier.

Learning could make time spent here seem worthwhile; so I will conduct short courses in first aid and medics to those who are interested. I will train whom I can at every opportunity. Sport and fitness must also be implemented to keep idle men happy. All officers and NCOs must take an interest in the men, or their effectiveness will be impaired. I realize this now, from seeing and living it, and this is what I should have learned at Gwelo. I hope next time to do better .

God has blessed me with fellowship here when loneliness has crept in. Life is much more enjoyable and endurable with friends, but I feel so alienated from those I know in Salisbury. It would be so nice to have a loving and understanding wife to return to, but I am getting used to being alone again, as I was in Gwelo. Still, it is not good. What a difference it would make just to have someone say, "Welcome back. I missed you, and I am happy to see you again."

Idleness and complacency are the greatest enemies of witness and achievement.

Although I am satisfied in my present work, and glad to be doing it, I feel no joy in it. This is wrong. Sometimes it is difficult to smile, even though I am happy, but this happiness is not complete.

6 November 1974

I've returned to Salisbury for a week, and I am having difficulty in my endeavours to become a Fireforce medic, because of the shortage of medics in the RLI. There are not enough to serve the commandos, the Support Group and the hospital, to spare me specifically for Fireforce.

I will, however, go to Mount Darwin to serve as such on my two weeks off, and to sort out something with the RLI commanding officer, Lieutenant-Colonel David Parker. If I cannot be there fulltime, perhaps he can influence the sub-unit OCs to let their medics go with the sticks, as I do with the Support Group.

I hope to improve the image of the commando medic, by making him an infantryman, what the Medical Corpsman is in the Marines. This will make the men proud of the Medical Corps and boost the confidence and morale of the troops, and save lives. I am staking my own life on this. It is my endeavour to make my own service in this army make a difference, to show that the medic is a better soldier. It is my way of saying that Rhodesia must fight, even if it means death. It is my example of Christian service. I must succeed in this, or my years in this army will be of no significance.

11 November 1974

Today is Independence Day for Rhodesia, the ninth anniversary of UDI. I've carried through with my plan and have returned to Mount Darwin, where I am on Fireforce standby with 1 Commando.

Things got off badly, for when I tried to explain the situation and what I wanted to do to the battalion adjutant, Captain Richard Lockley, he only replied, "Bullshit," and made an obscene gesture for me to leave. I went to the 'King' (Lieutenant-Colonel Parker*), who called through and sorted things out for me. There is still a bit of animosity and mistrust of an outsider from Support Group suddenly thrusting into 1 Commando.

* The nickname of 'The King' was testimony to the immense popularity David Parker enjoyed as CO of the RLI. A month after leaving the RLI in November 1975, he was tragically killed, together with four other members of the security forces, when the helicopter in which they were flying crashed. They had been on a goodwill tour visiting troops to wish them well for Christmas. He was thirty-eight years old.

I hope and trust that all will go well, and that God will grant His blessing on this effort to persuade the sub-unit OCs to place their commando medics in sticks on Fireforce where they are needed. To demonstrate this need, I must prove my worth again in a contact. I trust God and pray for a success. I can't afford a failure now.

[The journals were censored from 11 November to 26 December 1974. This period is filled in with letters written home and a taped message.]

21 November 1974

I have returned to the front again, after a week in camp. I decided to forego my time off, so I could come back to Mount Darwin. This is the best place to be for action and experience, and it has been worth coming here.

I had some difficulty in getting the position I wanted, but I managed. I am now a medic for whatever commando of the RLI is acting as Fireforce. I have been here since 11 November, Independence Day, and will carry on until after Christmas.

While 1 Commando was here we had two successful engagements, killing eleven terrs and capturing some, with no casualties of our own. A civilian African was wounded, and I managed to save him by doing a cut-down on his ankle so I could find a vein to insert the drip-set to replace his body fluids. I worked after dark by flashlight, staying up all night to keep him alive, until he could be casevaced the next morning.

No sooner had I returned from that scene, than fourteen Africans were brought into the hospital from an accident in which the truck they were riding rolled, crushing many of them. It was quite a grim scene. Two died in the hospital, and two others had to have legs amputated.

It is a challenge to work with a new unit in which you are virtually unknown, and to win the confidence, trust, and respect of the troops as a soldier and medic. I accomplished this goal in eight days with 1 Commando, and I am now working with 2 Commando.

As the crisis develops, we are all learning to fight, and so far we have been very successful militarily. Fortunately, the immediate enemy is not determined or well-trained, or our casualties would be much higher.

I hope for a miracle in this country. It is doubtful, but there is still hope.

When I finish this tour of duty, I think that at least in this battalion, which does the bulk of the fighting, that the medics will become like the Medical Corpsmen in the US forces. I am the first of what are now called 'combat medics' here. There will be others; so I have accomplished something.

I hope to make a tape for you when I return. In the meantime, I am happy here, and at this moment wouldn't be anywhere else. I sense God's intervention in this for me, and it will help me to achieve other aims later on.

7 December 1974

I am still at Mount Darwin on Fireforce where I have been seeing lots of action, more than most in this army. I would not trade this position for any other.

More effort has been taken to kill off or drive out the terrs, and every day we have gone out and slain many. We have had no serious casualties ourselves, although one man was killed today in another theatre of action. I have been fortunate in being able to go out every time with these men to fight, enabling me to fulfil my mission as combat soldier, medic, and witness for Christ.

We have succeeded militarily. Yet, as we anticipated, our success may be thrown away by the politicians. For today's news headlines tell of a possible ceasefire between the forces and the terrorist organizations – the results of the new détente between South Africa and Zambia. Not being optimistic, I fear this will lead to compromises and eventual surrender. The beginning of the end.

This area has changed so much since the rains. Everything looks so green and beautiful and pastoral. It is hard to believe it is the scene of so much killing.

I may be here for a week or another three weeks. I hope the latter, because I am fulfilling my mission here for this period of my life. God has blessed us exceedingly and has protected us.

It has been impossible for me to get Christmas cards, so I will wish you a very Happy Christmas now, and God's blessing for next year.

22 December 1974

The past few weeks have been very eventful for Rhodesia. As a result of negotiations between South Africa and Zambia (but also including Rhodesia), a ceasefire has been called between the terrorist groups and the security forces. This may halt the flow of incoming terrs for a while, but we must still deal with those already here. Attempts have been made to get them to surrender by radio broadcasts, leaflet dropping, and sky-shouts. The latter involves playing tapes over loudspeakers from airplanes, usually Dakotas. For us, things are the same, and we remain on standby. Although action has quietened down a bit, we still get called out.

In yesterday's assault my helicopter was shot down as we were landing. The pilot was hit in the knee and we nearly crashed, but the pilot was able to bring us down safely.

I have now been on more combat callouts than most in this army, and I would not hesitate to go at any time, although I get scared in every contact. I know I am completely in God's hands, and I trust Him to look after me until such time as my purpose in this world is finished.

There is reason to be optimistic, as Black Africa is starving now, and Rhodesia and South Africa have food to export. We have the upper hand and have won a military victory, which has placed the prime minister in a strong position from which to bargain. Let us hope he uses it wisely and does not throw our success away.

My tour of duty will be over in a week, when I hope to get plenty of much-needed time off. I feel I have accomplished what I set out to do, which was to get combat medics into the field with the troops, and create a better impression of Christians in this army.

I hope to come back here again soon and carry on, but I need a rest. I've been sick the past two days, but I'm getting better now. I could just use a break.

I wish you a very Merry Christmas and Happy New Year. Maybe next year I can get home.

CHAPTER 29
Lonely Christmas in Salisbury

26 December 1974

On Monday, after six weeks on Fireforce, I was recalled to Salisbury, only to be redeployed with 2 Commando the following Sunday.

I feel my objective was achieved, for, although we had no serious casualties, the need for combat medics was demonstrated and proven. Now the troop medics in RLI will be retrained as next year for that very purpose.

I am the first; so I feel I have had an influence in the army. I have increased my experience and improved my reputation, and feel that I have lived down my ignominious demise from the SAS. I have truly become a veteran of this war.

Coming back to town was a shock for me, however. I could not fit in with the civilians I know, and I feel increasingly alienated from them. I feel that I need a wife, someone to come home to, but I have none. By Christmas Eve I felt so completely and utterly alone, I could only break down and cry.

I visited the parents of friends in Que Que on Christmas, but they were not much help. I was very uncongenial and unfriendly. I cannot believe that God intends for me not to have a wife. One would be such a help to me now, but I've borne my latest emotional crisis alone.

December 1974

[Taped Christmas message sent home]

For the army there are terrorist gangs still roaming around the countryside that have to be eliminated. So there are still contacts, although the influx of terrorists may subside temporarily. But let it be known that whenever terrorist gangs or conventional forces cross these borders, there are many of us here who are willing to go out and to meet them at any time, at any place, and destroy them.

My own involvement in these events over the last several months has enabled me to make a very effective witness to the troops here. It has been my experience that a Christian soldier who, by his actions, shows that he can soldier better than any other troops because of his religious convictions, has a far more effective witness than if he just speaks of personal beliefs about Jesus Christ or platitudes about righteous living. Not only have I been able to bring the message of Christ to individuals, but also I've been commander at the memorial services we have had for our dead. And every Christian who enters the armed forces must realize that if his beliefs and his witness are to be respected, he must first prove himself to be a soldier and a man.

A Christian soldier has much to fight for in this country. I always like to think of the words of the German Crusader, Count Volkmar, who spoke on the eve of his departure to the Holy Land back in 1197: "Let it be known that I am marching to Jerusalem because the work of God should be respected in this world, and because the scenes in which our Saviour, the Lord Jesus, lived should not fall into pagan hands. I am marching with a goodly band and we have placed ourselves entirely into the hands of God. For we go forth as servants to accomplish His will."

Although it is popular today to ridicule the Crusades, we need the same spiritual drive and religious motivation of our ancestors if we are to survive the crisis facing the Western world today. Rhodesia is the last place on the face of the earth where there remains a vestige of the old colonial life-style and culture. Once gone here, it will vanish forever, making it one of the world's great tragedies if it happens. Although this culture may have its flaws, at least Christianity is still practised here and evangelism is undertaken freely, enabling thousands to hear the Gospel, who otherwise might never hear it.

It is also wise to remember that all those other former colonies granted 'independence' have since fallen under a far more ruthless imperialism of Western corporations, communists, and Zionists, than was ever known under a benign colonialism.

Many pray for the safety of those who fight in the bush, and this is needed and very much appreciated. But we must expect many to be hurt and killed because we are at war with implacable enemies. Let us pray instead for the success and victory which can be achieved, lest those already killed have died in vain.

It is Scriptural to fight; listen to the Epistle of James: "Resist the devil and he will flee from you." And that applies to all the devil's manifestations in the world, such as communism.

Remember the appeal of Nehemiah as the Hebrews wept over the ruins of the nation: "Be ye not afraid of them. Remember that the Lord which is great and terrible would have you fight for your brothers, your sons, your daughters, your wives, and for your houses."

The words of Moses apply to us too: "If I shall say in my heart these nations are more than I, how can I dispossess them? Thou shalt not be afraid of them, but shall remember what the Lord did unto all Egypt and shall chase your enemy and they shall fall before you by the sword."

Many are the forces abroad which wish to plunder Rhodesia and South Africa for the wealth of natural resources here, and for the strategic location of the Cape watching over the oil routes from the Middle East. These enemies are pushing terrorism on us. They are applying psychopolitics to try to undermine our faith in ourselves, and they are directing world opinion against us. We must require that spirit of heroism against which no material force can prevail. Nothing can defeat that except inner decadence. And we must require the will to fight, even when there is no apparent hope, and even if it means death. And like the Crusader, Volkmar, we must seek to accomplish God's will and to place ourselves entirely in His hands. Only then will we find Victory, and then can we keep these lands from pagan hands.

[The journals, from 26 December 1974 to 19 July 1975, the day of John's death, were censored or destroyed. The following were letters written by John.]

22 January 1975

Sorry about the delay in writing, but the past few weeks have been very hectic. The commando unit I'm with now has been very mobile, moving wherever we were most needed.

We were in the Zambezi Valley again for a while. That is the real Africa of tropical heat, wild animals, junglechoked valleys, and truly primitive tribesmen. Very interesting to see but uncomfortable to be in. Many men came down with malaria, in spite of prophylaxis, and we were exposed to a multitude of tropical diseases like sleeping sickness. We have left there now, and I've taken over many other responsibilities as several of the other NCOs are sick. I'm glad to be as healthy as ever.

I was doing Fireforce again, only in another area, but we had only one contact. Terrorist groups are reported to have re-entered the country, so we will not be unemployed. Constitutional talks are to be held shortly, in which the government is supposed to reach some kind of settlement as we continue the fighting. This may be the sell-out I've anticipated. I will have to decide soon whether to stay on.

Russian arms are beginning to pour into Beira harbour in Mozambique, and we shall face those in the near future. Chinese 'diplomats' have been welcomed into Botswana. Yesterday one of the Support Group sergeants was seriously injured in a landmine blast. Many are willing to fight on, no matter what the odds, if only they have the chance.

The incident in December was not really a crash, just an abrupt landing with a lot of lead flying. The pilot was hit and the rest of us were shaken up. In the other crash, where three were killed, I knew the casevaced patient.

I was really sorry to see the major of this sub-unit transferred. He was its life and spirit, one of those you would follow to hell and back. Certainly one of the best field majors I've met. Since he has gone, the personality clashes between officers and NCOs have caused havoc.

I'll be going back to Salisbury again in a few days when I'll have time to listen to the Christmas tape you sent. I want to go to Bulawayo for a couple of weeks to complete another medics' course and to visit friends there.

I'm so glad you all had an enjoyable and eventful Christmas with a guest from Rhodesia in our home. From Antoinette's (Fourie) letters, she seems to have thoroughly enjoyed her visit with you. She and I agree on some things, but not all of us are called to serve God in the same way. Her parents have been good to me, and I go there when I am in Que Que. However, I find that I have difficulty when I come back from the bush now, adjusting to the civilian world again. It is because of an increasing alienation from people who just don't know what it is all about.

CHAPTER 30
Back to Mount Darwin

20 February 1975

As we have been anticipating, the United States is experiencing economic chaos resulting from decades of inflation and deficit spending. Now it has hit you personally. Unless I am really needed at home, I will stay on here. The economic crisis has not been felt here yet, although Australia is hard hit also. So it will probably be worldwide as it was in the 1930s. Rhodesia has far less to lose economically.

If I don't write as much as I once did, it is because the novelty and excitement of a new way of life has grown old, but I assure you that I will keep you informed of all my plans, activities, and appraisal of the situation here, as it unfolds.

I have been kept busy in the camp hospital since coming back from Malawi. While in Salisbury, I've spent several evenings visiting those I haven't seen in months. Most seem to still have faith in their national leaders.

With the exodus of the Portuguese Mozambique is deteriorating rapidly. Rhodesia isn't lost yet, but it is disappointing to see talks being held with criminals. I don't think much will come of these sessions, particularly since the ceasefire has become obviously ludicrous. In a few days I'll be at Mount Darwin again, and it will be good to get out of camp and back to the bush.

I was pleased to see a particular letter in the *South African Observer* criticizing Rhodesia's attitude of dètente. You should know who wrote it.

It is regrettable that the US will not allow any parcels sent from Rhodesia to enter the US. There are things I would like to send you, now that I can afford to buy them. It is apparent that not all of your letters get through to me, and I'm sure not all of mine reach you.

I am considering going into forestry over here, so please send my forestry notebooks from Ohio State University, and also my army gloves for winter. Thanks.

The Lutheran hymnal and the text on Christian doctrine that you sent me for Christmas are really precious. I am reminded of our Christian heritage when I follow Pastor Lang's sermons on the tapes.

2 March 1975

Many thanks for the Christmas pictures that arrived this week. I enjoyed them very much. As you probably know by now, I am at Mount Darwin, my favourite location on Fireforce.

There is still much hope here, as I see it, which is why I carry on. The clippings I sent you will testify to this, for there are many Rhodesians who understand the score. Some articles, however, came from the liberal *Rhodesia Herald* newspaper, one of the Argus Press group of Harry Oppenheimer.

As you are aware, much of our struggle is a conflict of psychological warfare. Many articles are planted in the press to undermine our faith and confidence.

Although I am often discouraged and come to the point where I want to give up fighting for causes and ideals, I realize that such despair would be a personal defeat for me, a killing of my own soul.

I hope to see the outcome of it all, and it will be a sad day for me if I have to leave Africa. As long as I can help to fight our enemies – European or American liberals, white, black, or yellow communists – I want to be a part of the struggle.

I empathize with the people caught up in all this: the soldiers, police, farmers, and all. I have not made many friends, because people pass into and out of my life, and then I never see them again. Sometimes it is with regret, other times with relief.

I wish you a happy birthday, Mom. I love you and wish you God's blessing.

13 March 1975

Two of your letters came through. While I'm in the bush my mail accumulates at the hospital, until someone decides to send it out.

I especially appreciate the book *A Summary of Christian Doctrine* and the old Lutheran hymnal. Now I can follow the sequence of the church year and read the Lenten passages, since I rarely have an opportunity to attend church.

Today we are halfway through our stay here, and we have not had much success yet. One of our trucks hit a mine, and the back wheel was blown off. No one was hurt badly, just one chap with a burst eardrum. Another unit was ambushed, with three wounded and one dead. I didn't personally know any of them.

I went on an ambush myself last week. We had everything going for us, but our information proved a bit stale, as happens ninety-nine percent of the time in ambushes. No luck and no terrs showed up. If they had, nine shotguns would have blasted them to kingdom come. Yesterday we were called out to attack a terrorist camp. We found it, but the terrs had gone, leaving not a trace to indicate their direction. So that's how it's been going. The ceasefire last December has set us back many months. Some of the political detainees released should then be rearrested.

The planned constitutional conference hasn't materialized yet, since the conferees cannot even agree on a place to hold it. I'm not sorry about that though.

Another American here has made a good analogy to this war (if it can be called that): Rhodesian tactics are more like what the US army was doing on the Mexican border just before World War I, chasing Pancho Villa and his bandits around New Mexico and Arizona.

20 March 1975

I can understand your feelings, as parents, for my safety, but I will keep going back to the bush again, again, and again, until I am satisfied that I have the combat experience I want. It isn't anything at all like Vietnam, where there was heavy fighting every day. I felt unlucky that this time I missed the two big punch-ups we had. I was near, but got there a day late for each. I am not reckless now as I was a few months ago, because I know what can happen. I also have the confidence that God is looking after me and will keep me safe anywhere for as long as He wills, and for whatever reasons or purposes.

There are other reasons why I stay in the combat zone. The war in this country is much more psychological and psycho-political than military, and the former is where we are losing. I become very depressed and demoralized when there are so few who encourage us and remind us of what we are fighting for. Morale in the army is very low, and our generals and politicians, with the exception of President Dupont and the former defence minister, have done nothing, or said nothing to encourage or to bolster it. This is where we are defeated, not from lack of willingness to fight.

Major General Rawlings visited us here today. Do you think he said anything at all to boost our morale? He could only mumble something about what we do all day when we are not on call.

Any authority I have to speak or write, encouraging a will and determination to win, to fight, and to expose the enemy, comes from my active involvement in the war. Only then will anyone listen to me, when I do more than they have to, when I don't have to do it at all. If we look for guidance, leadership, and encouragement in others, we will be mostly disappointed, as I have been. So we must provide it within ourselves, from our own faith, determination, and understanding of the situation. Actions speak louder than words and are needed to make what words are spoken effective.

There is something else that makes me stay on here and which has kept me from going before now. That is the bond with the troops with whom I serve. No one ever talks about it much, especially among the Rhodesians and South Africans of Afrikaner stock, but there is a bulldog-like determination to fight on, no matter what the odds, and that is the hope see for southern Africa. As long as there are people like the farmers I meet, who leave their fields two or three months a year to fight with us, I am willing to do it full time.

I am a professional soldier, a commando, and a paratrooper. All my training has been for this. Unlike some who come here looking for adventure and action, I am here out of personal commitment and fulfilment of a destiny that is yet obscure. I cannot leave until am satisfied that it is completed.

I do not know how much longer I will be on the front.

If my application for medical school is approved, then it will only be until November of this year. If not, then the best course will be to complete my contract and to carry on until October 1976, when I can take all the leave I have accumulated. But I cannot decide on this until June. In the meantime, I soldier on, trying to contribute what I can personally, trying to bolster morale, and trying to make an effective Christian witness. Sometimes my deep state of depression nullifies these attempts.

I may transfer to another unit, the Selous Scouts, or may even go back to the SAS, but my company commander does not want to lose me from the commando.

I went down into the valley on an ambush last week. We missed the terrs, but the SAS nailed them, killing fourteen out of twenty-five. One SAS trooper was killed, and a corporal wounded by an accidental discharge. The next day, in another engagement, one of the Support Group officers was wounded in a contact, but he is recovering well. These casualties support my case for having combat medics from the Medical Corps with the troops at all times. It seems that I am still the only one.

Many Portuguese soldiers have fled Mozambique and are joining us. Some are ex-Frelimo who went over to the Portuguese and had to flee for their lives.

Thanks for being such wonderful parents. I love you so much.

30 March 1975

Hi, again, and Happy Easter. I'll write this now while I have the chance, before reporting for operations again.

It has been a very good week, not having to work and being able to rest up. This Easter hasn't been very good spiritually. Not that it has lost its meaning for me in any way, but in times like this I really miss our traditional Lutheran services.

I'll be going to Salisbury this afternoon, then on to the bush tomorrow for another month. I don't even know where we are going this time, but it will be as a high-intensity force, which means that we move all over the operational areas, reacting to all intelligence reports and incidents.

15 April 1975

Operations were eventful this time, although things are quite dull at the moment. Three days after we left, we had a good contact, but took a hard knock when one of the patrol groups was caught in an ambush, leaving one officer and two RAR trackers killed, and one of our guys wounded. The officer had just been commissioned, and this was his first time out on operations. I was choppered in to recover the wounded man, gave him first aid at the scene, and then transported him to where a helicopter could lift him out. The ambush was in a deep ravine in thick bush, so it wasn't an easy task or very pretty. But we did capture some terr leaders and found arms caches.

There are talks being held in Dar es Salaam this week between African so-called 'heads of state', the guerrilla leaders, and Vorster. Ndabaningi Sithole, leader of ZANU (Zimbabwe African National Union), the terrorist organization we are fighting now, was released from detention to attend it, just after he was reconvicted for conspiracy. Hopefully he won't come back so that the taxpayers won't be paying his upkeep. He won't do much harm outside the country.

29 April 1975

This time I've been out for more than four weeks. I played a key role in our recent 'psyops' (psychological operations) to win hearts and minds by treating cases of malaria among tribesmen. I was able to save one of our own guys who had an allergy to a bee sting.

We had a group of former Portuguese army servicemen working with us. They are African, white, and Coloured. All of them had been fighting in Angola and Mozambique, and they fled to Rhodesia after the communist takeover of Portugal and the sell-out of the African colonies. They have been branded as 'criminals' there, but are now working for us. They have been posted into various units, and when we went to the border post of Mukumbura, they were left behind – deliberately – to prevent a clash with a company of Frelimo on the Mozambique side.

Because of détente we must avoid any confrontation with roving communist bands, in spite of all the action we had with them before. Our one great weapon that could be used against Marxist Africa is starvation. Yet we send food to Mozambique and Zambia, just as the United States always feeds the Soviet Union.

Although my continued military service here seems, more often than not, futile and frustrating, for the time being it is well to carry on with it for the insight it gives. I gain something every time I take a tour of duty. I like to compare my years of military and combat experience to what I might have known had I served during one of the world wars.

The South African police pulled out of Rhodesia last week. We escorted one company from their basecamp to the paved road to see them off. It isn't much of a loss to us, because we need regular troops, not police.

So you are having spring now. The spring and autumn months of April and September were always my favourite time at home. It is the African autumn here and very invigorating. The leaves do not change colour as at home. They just turn brown and drop off.

Greetings again from the hemisphere of the Southern Cross. The happy hunter has returned once again to the bright lights of Salisbury. I have two weeks off and intend to recoup and reappraise the whole situation.

I've been on the brink of moral collapse for some time now. What I mean by that is that I feel that I've had enough playing around at war. Since I enjoy the African bush, and now feel at home there, the cities have lost their appeal. However, as we all have anticipated, politics have frustrated that moral intent and purpose which led me there. I haven't lost it, but increasingly, I just don't give a damn any more. Denied the right of command, I've tried to show leadership by my own involvement and commitment in operations. I hope that, if there is to be any fighting, it will come soon, while I can still have a part of it before my time runs out.

It is encouraging to know that détente is on the verge of collapse now. Perhaps now we can get back to the straight confrontation that we all love. For then there is certainty.

Rhodesia's unforgivable sin, I believe, is that it does nothing to help the white revolt which was suppressed in Mozambique. The current friendly attitude toward Frelimo is suicidal for us. We conducted operations against them up until just last year, but now we have to avoid any confrontation with them. We have even been pulled back on occasions to avoid a punch-up. That is what has disappointed me the most.

Civil war is brewing in Angola and Portugal itself. A situation like the Congo, or even the Spanish Civil War, may develop. Several Portuguese veterans from Angola and Mozambique have joined us, but some want to return to fight again in Angola.

Internationalist pressure from South Africa has played havoc with us. It is terribly ironic to think that Vorster was put in detention during World War II for his nationalist views.

It is frightening to see the great communist advances so recently: the fall of Portugal, Mozambique and Angola, and the capture of Saigon on May Day, marking the fall of South Vietnam. Like the French, we can say, "We never lost; we were always betrayed."

CHAPTER 31
The Final Weeks

7 May 1975

Here I am in Salisbury again and I will have most of the time off for three weeks. I had planned to stay at Karanda Mission to help a doctor I know there. It is near Mount Darwin, and I had hoped to get some terrs on my own there, but the plan did not work out. So I've been hanging around Salisbury, just taking it easy and doing more writing.

The big news around here is the Commonwealth Conference in Jamaica, where all the black Marxists are calling for the final reduction of Rhodesia by more sanctions and military force. This is good news, for then perhaps we can have an end to détente, and have the security of a straightforward confrontation.

This has been a great year for communism, indeed, now that the takeover is complete in Portugal, Mozambique, and all of south-east Asia. A friend of mind made a good point: "It cannot be compared with just anti-communism. A deeper and much more spiritual movement is needed, with a new alter African, not just the negation of communism."

I have applied again for medical school, which will determine when I leave the army. I also applied for Rhodesian citizenship, which will take a few weeks to process. I can still retain my US passport, and I am not giving up my United States citizenship. I will be a dual citizen of the two republics. The US Jews are allowed to hold dual citizenship for both the United States and Israel, so that they can go to Israel to fight for the Zionist cause. Therefore, I can hold dual citizenship also.

The prospect of civil war in Angola increases, making a market for mercenaries there imminent.

Happy Mother's Day, Mom. I hope the flowers arrive.

Thanks for being such great parents to me.

23 May 1975

As you have probably guessed, I am on operations again, but this time it has been more like an unexpected holiday. We have gone to the resort area of Kariba, and it is really fantastic. I've been posted to a basecamp, but there is very little military action. I've never seen big game in such abundance. There are herds of elephants,

Cape buffalo, hippo, and impala, which come right by our camp. But they come at night when I can't take pictures.

My prospects for medical school fell through. I would have to pay all tuition fees and expenses on my monthly salary of $100, a route I'm not prepared to take again. I still feel that I have a destiny and a fulfilment as a soldier to achieve, and twenty-two months left to do it in. I came close to it last December but was cut short. So I am waiting for another opportunity. Sitting here is all very pleasant, but it is not what I want to spend my time doing. I will wait a few more months to see how things develop. At least I have some renewed confidence in Ian Smith, now that détente has virtually collapsed in southern Africa. But there is still considerable danger from Vorster and the internationalists who control him. I must just wait for the next terrorist assault to come, as it most probably will.

Depending on how things go, I may take leave over Christmas, or I may just wait until the end of winter. I am only permitted a maximum of two months' leave at a time. When I return from this op at Kariba, I will inquire into forestry positions. I would like to stay in southern Africa, but only if I can work in the bush and away from the cities. I trust God's guidance in this. He will show me the way and what I must do.

I hope to tour South Africa later and, hopefully, South West Africa too, if I can afford it. I have some really good friends now, both well-informed and Christians, who have made life more pleasant for me.

7 June 1975

I just returned to Salisbury today, and I feel the cold weather now, especially after being at Kariba on the Zambezi.

This last trip seemed like a waste of time because nothing was achieved militarily. However, it was enjoyable to visit a new area I haven't seen before. The next operation should be better, back in the old hunting grounds at Darwin.

Don't give up on my coming home yet. I know it has been a long time. I don't want to leave until I am satisfied with my own military achievement. These past few months have been gruelling for me, but things are shaping up now.

There were riots again in Salisbury this week, and the crunch is coming. I want to be here when it comes. It has become the focal point of my life, my part in history.

My role as a medic is to give first aid in the field for war injuries, to treat what sicknesses I can, and to casevac serious cases. I can also do minor operations such as suturing wounds. The rest is straight soldiering.

Acknowledgement from John's family

The last letter written by John, to his parents and brother, in June 1975 while on his leave in South Africa, was not received. We give our heartfelt thanks to Louis Fourie Jnr of Bulawayo, Rhodesia; Antoinette Fourie of Que Que, Rhodesia, then in Dallas, Texas; and Dr Gilbert Douglas of Birmingham, Alabama, for giving us their letters from John – among the last ever written by our beloved son and brother.

10 June 1975

John's letter to Antoinette Fourie:
Hello, how are you? I regret not to have written sooner, but lost your address again, and I was at Bumi Hills on Lake Kariba for three weeks. That was a good change from our usual stomping grounds, but it was a waste of time. It was fun cruising across the lake and watching the herds of elephant, buffalo, zebra and impala.

Last Saturday your brother Louis left for the bush on PATU [Police Anti-terrorist Unit] patrol for two weeks. I met him at the train station then took him to your sister's flat for breakfast. He was surprised to see me there. I wish he were stationed in Salisbury.

I went down to Pretoria, South Africa, as I'd been wanting to renew my passport. I visited with your grandparents in Louis Trichardt for one night, and enjoyed staying there. Being in that old house was like travelling back decades in time. Your *oupa* (grandfather) must stay in bed and is slowly losing his sight. It was fascinating talking with him. He told me of his experiences fighting Germans and Kaffirs in South West Africa during World War I when he was a soldier. It is not often that one can hear a first-hand account of something that long ago. Your *ouma* (grandmother) was really super too.

Fortunately, I had no trouble getting a new passport, in spite of the fact that I am in a foreign army, with sworn allegiance to Rhodesia. What a chuckle, filling out those papers under a portrait of Henry Kissinger.

I've been staying in Pretoria with the parents of one of my mates, who live near a prison. It is quite likely that I'll be on the other side of those walls one day when the power-hungry Vorster puts his conservative adversaries and critics in detention, while he ruins Western civilization in Rhodesia and South Africa. No doubt he will soon sell out South West Africa.

This is the month Frelimo is handed complete control of Mozambique. Civil war is still raging in Angola.

I was right in my anticipation of what would happen at Karanda Mission. About twenty armed terrs went there one night and demanded that Dr Drake give them medical supplies and support. The missionaries all had quite a fright. Pity I wasn't there as I wanted to be. If there was any doubt about whose side TEAM missionaries were on before, there is none now.

I still have a plan I must discuss with Colonel Parker, if he will let me go there.

All I am hoping, praying, and waiting for now is a piece of the action again, so that I can have the satisfaction and peace of mind of knowing that my time in Rhodesia and the army was worthwhile and made a difference. It has already, I know. There are fellows walking around who would be dead if I hadn't been there, but I'm not satisfied with just that.

8 July 1975

John's last letter to reach home:

Once again, I am playing my favourite role as Fireforce medic, but we have had only a few call-outs and no contacts as yet, although the company here before us had some. We could close this up quickly if the politicians would let us hit the enemy camps in Mozambique. We know where they are. A battalion attack would smash them. In the meantime we sit and wait, practise PT and quick-kill shooting, and I give lessons on medics and first aid. It seems I've heard that tune before.

There is not much to write about since I wrote of my trip to South Africa in my last letter. But perhaps you didn't receive it. [The letter was not received.]

One request, if you could please send the book *The Genesis Flood*, as I want it for a friend of mine who is a schoolteacher and does not want to teach evolution. That book would be a big help.

10 July 1975

John's letter to Dr Douglas:

Thanks very much for the unexpected letter. It is very much appreciated, particularly since my contacts in America have been reduced to only three outside my own family. In fact, the only ties I have remaining with my homeland after four years' absence are precariously bound by weekly letters.

I am content staying in Rhodesia, but I plan on taking three months' leave next year in April, May, and June. I will go home to see how things are before deciding definitely on settling here. It is good to hear of your activities and concern. I'll most certainly try to meet you all when I return home, particularly since my brother is in your area. I have friends in Baton Rouge and Dallas who I hope to see.

What is the attraction here for me and with what can I compare it? The first Europeans arrived here only eighty years ago; so Rhodesia has only been settled for a few generations. If one journeys outside the cities, it becomes very obvious that this is the frontier of Western civilization. The lifestyle is somewhat colonial, although many who have been here for decades say that it is nothing like it once was.

Rhodesia is a product of the British Empire. Less than 100 years ago, the British overcame the Zulu opposition, and eighty years ago that of the Matabele. Now we are at the other end of the sine curve, or cycle of history, clinging to the last remnant of that great Empire. If nothing else, I can say I fought for the last of the old, colonial empires, such as the Portuguese only so recently lost.

The insurgency we are counteracting now does not amount to a guerrilla movement, since the terrorists against whom we are operating are not that good. They are in a class far below the Viet Cong, although both are trained by the same communists. That is the difference between Africans and Asians. It is more like the action on the Mexican border before World War I, or similar to the way in which the Indians attacked the white farmers on the old frontier. Where else could one find mounted infantry still in operation, modelling themselves on the dragoons and hussars of the last century?

Then there is the real Africa of the Zambezi Valley, and places in Mozambique still devoid of any human life, with nothing but bush and herds of wild animals. Perhaps it was in this environment, and not in suburban America, that I became a man. I feel more a part of this scene and more committed here than I ever did in America. However, you may be right. It is probably just the loss of contact. So many people have become a disappointment when

I see them use Christianity as an escape and a cop out. They use it as an escape from the hell on earth that they permit to develop by default. Don't misunderstand me, I have still retained my faith in Jesus Christ.

15 July 1975

John's letter to Louis Fourie, Jnr:

Greetings from the Khe Sanh [battle in Vietnam in 1968] of Op *Hurricane*. I've been here for the last three weeks in my favourite role on Fireforce, but it has really been a farce so far.

We've had only about five call-outs, all of them fruitless, and only a few killed in ambushes. Last Saturday night I accompanied a pregnant mother, caught in crossfire, on a casevac back to the hospital in Salisbury. She survived, but her foetus was dead, aborted I presume. What an irony, that a child is killed by gunshot wounds in war, even before it is born.

I've been trying to keep from stagnating from the inactivity. There are hundreds of terrs around here, but we just don't seem to get onto them now. The SAS just had a contact tonight, so hopefully we will get some before we go back next week.

I had a scheme to catch some terrs at Karanda Mission that the commanding officer approved. He would have sent me, but the head missionary there objected when he approached him on it, thwarting the whole thing. That was really disappointing.

The RLI is being granted the Freedom of Salisbury* when we return, and also of Victoria Falls. I'll be here again on Fireforce in August and September. So if you are here, look me up.

[This was John's last letter]

* Rhodesian Light Infantry was granted the Freedom of the capital on 25 July 1975.

CHAPTER 32
The Last Battle

The following is an accurate account of John's death by former RLI Trooper David S. Armstrong, as related in a letter dated 9 September 1985. David was at the scene:

> 2 Commando, RLI, was based at Mount Darwin on Fireforce duties, and on 19 July, 7-Troop was on first wave – that is, the first to respond to a call for assistance by troops on patrol in the bush. As commando medic, John was in Lieutenant Johannes 'Joe' du Plooy's stick of four.
>
> During the morning, a TA [Territorial Army, in this case elements of 2nd Battalion, the Rhodesia Regiment] patrol had been ambushed by a group of six terrorists, and in the ensuing contact, the TAs managed to kill two terrorists. The remainder broke and ran.
>
> As there was no immediate prospect of regaining contact with the terrorists, 7-Troop was not called upon to respond immediately. The result was that Corporal Johannes 'Jannie' de Beer of 10-Troop was deployed with his stick to assist the TA patrol follow up the tracks of the terrorists, since de Beer was an experienced tracker. (I should explain what a 'stick' is. A stick is the term used internationally to designate the body of troops deployed by aircraft. In our case we were using Alouette III helicopters and thus a stick consisted of four troops. When using a Dakota (DC-3) a stick consisted of about eighteen to twenty troops.)
>
> Several hours later, 7-Troop was called out as the combined TA and 10-Troop stick had been ambushed in a narrow, twisty, overgrown riverbed, or *donga*. The *donga* was about ten feet deep and not much wider, with heavily overgrown banks which were very precipitous. In one particular section of the river, there were two sharp bends, about twenty to twenty-five yards apart. In the outside bank of the second bend, there was a washout fronted by heavy tree roots. It was in this extremely strong natural position that the terrorists had taken position. They had two major advantages, and these were that it was very difficult for anyone to see into this washout without exposing himself in full view to enemy fire. In fact,

it was more than difficult; it was impossible. The second major advantage was the fact that the floor of the washout was about two feet above the level of the riverbed.

The combined TA and 10-Troop stick had come around the first bend, and in doing so exposed themselves to the terrorists, who opened fire. The tracker, Warrant Officer Tazewil 'Taz' Bain of the TA patrol, and a member of Corporal de Beer's stick, Rifleman Eben 'Hennie' Potgieter, were both killed. Ken Lucas, the gunner in Corporal de Beer's stick, was wounded in the legs.

It was into this situation that 7-Troop arrived. Major 'Hank' Meyer deployed Lieutenant du Plooy's stick with another to sweep through the area, as at this stage no-one was sure whether the terrorists were still there or not. The figures of the two soldiers in the riverbed were seen by this sweep line, so Lieutenant du Plooy ordered John to see if he could help them. As John climbed down into the riverbed, he was shot by the terrorists who were still in their hiding place – right under Lieutenant du Plooy's feet. [John was hit twice: a fatal shot to the brain and one to the heel.]

During the rest of the afternoon, several attempts were made to get at the terrorists in their position. This is where they used the strength of that position to their advantage. As I said before, anyone attempting to assault the position was clearly exposed, but at the same time unable to see into the target area. We suffered two more casualties, one of whom was Lieutenant du Plooy who was wounded. Also, any grenades thrown at the terrorists simply bounced off the tree roots fronting the position and exploded harmlessly on the sand of the riverbed.

My stick was deployed about thirty yards downstream from the main contact area as a stop group, and towards dark more troops were flown in to provide a tighter cordon. Shortly after dark, the four terrorists broke out. As they came out, they managed to kill Corporal de Beer and wound another of his stick. Again no-one was sure whether the terrorists had continued with their breakout, or had returned to their position in the riverbank.

The SAS* were asked for assistance as they were equipped with night sights, which we in the RLI didn't have, and towards midnight they were able to clear the position and confirm that the terrorists had escaped. Shortly afterwards, I assisted in retrieving John's body along with the others from the riverbed.

* American Vietnam veteran and recipient of the Purple Heart, Lieutenant Robert 'Bob' MacKenzie of the SAS had that night been following the events in the army operations' room in Mount Darwin. Realizing the situation had reached an impasse, he quickly rounded up several members of the squadron, and persuaded two air force helicopter pilots to take them to the scene in the Masoso TTL, north of Mount Darwin and close to the border with Mozambique.

An hour later they arrived and were quickly briefed by Corporal 'Butch' Alexander of the RLI who, in the absence of the wounded Lieutenant du Plooy, had assumed command of the situation. With two members of the SAS contingent providing cover with night sights fitted to their rifles, MacKenzie and Alexander crawled to the edge of the riverbank. In the moonlight they finally managed to see the three wounded men, Bain, Potgieter and Coey, lying close to each other on the riverbed. There was no movement from any of them.

There was, however, no way of knowing if the terrorists were still in their hideout, so MacKenzie had the RLI troops lob grenades, including white phosphorus, into the riverbed. This was followed by an extended period of firing into possible terrorists positions, but there was no return fire. Undaunted, and wishing to end the on-going uncertainty about the fate of the Rhodesian soldiers as well as the whereabouts of the terrorist stronghold, MacKenzie felt that the only remaining option was to go down into the riverbed. Taking one of his men, armed with an MAG, and Alexander, the latter insisting he had to go along to see to his fellow troops, MacKenzie stripped off his webbing and, leaving his rifle behind and armed only with a pistol and a grenade, entered the riverbed 150 metres downstream from the possible terrorist position.

With nerves at breakpoint, the trio inched their way along, the moonlight providing guiding visibility, but at the same time creating shadows and questionable shapes. Then suddenly, the palpable tension was broken, as the extremely loud clatter of bursts of fire from the MAG shattered the stillness. The MAG gunner, feeling uncomfortable about something ahead, fired over the heads of MacKenzie and Alexander, intermittent red tracer streaking towards the riverbank. Abrupt silence followed. But still no response from the terrorists.

Eventually the men reached their fallen comrades, their worst fears realized as they failed to find any traces of life in any of the three soldiers. MacKenzie was also able, at last, to identify the cave where the terrorists had been firing from, his eyes drawn to globules of white phosphorus burning on the walls of the cave. After lobbing further grenades into the cave, MacKenzie crept into the cave, only to find that the terrorists had made good their escape. The terrorists had escaped across a maize field and in between stop groups, taking with them the MAG and ammunition carried by one of the Rhodesian soldiers.

Tracking was made difficult for the SAS trackers the following morning, the terrorists tracks blending in with those of locals in the area. The MAG, however, was found, the heavy weapon abandoned by the fleeing terrorists. This marked the end of a tragic and frustrating engagement with terrorists, one which was typical of the nature of Rhodesia's bush war, the enemy taking full advantage of difficult and often treacherous terrain. Four lost their lives, but in all of this, the Rhodesian soldiers refused to give up on their brothers, unselfishly placing their own lives at great risk.

In his time with the SAS in Rhodesia, MacKenzie, who later became a captain, was awarded two of Rhodesia's top gallantry awards, the Silver Cross of Rhodesia (SCR) and the Bronze Cross of Rhodesia (BCR). MacKenzie was killed in an engagement with rebels in Sierra Leone on 24 February 1995. He had been hired by that country's government to assist with eliminating anti-government forces.

In my opinion, one unusual circumstance and two mistakes occurred which contributed to this fiasco. It was a fiasco as well as a great tragedy. I feel I must tell you them. The unusual circumstance was that the terrorists were well-led and prepared to fight it out. The RLI was definitely not prepared for this. The first mistake was that too many people were in the riverbed initially, and there was no flanking protection for the tracker. I can only assume that this was to enable the trackers to catch up with the terrorists and not be slowed down by having to wait for troops moving through the thick bush on either riverbank. The second mistake was that of Lieutenant du Plooy's in sending John into the riverbed without having completed the sweep of the area.

Incidentally, the terrorist leader was identified by the police Special Branch and we later heard that he had been killed by another unit. This would have been in 1976.

Lieutenant du Plooy was killed in 1979, when the helicopter he was in was shot down near Mapai in Mozambique. The riverbed contact was the worst single event of my three years with 2 Commando and the only one in which the terrorists got the better of us.

A Military Funeral

John Alan Coey was laid to rest on 28 July 1975, in the country for which he gave his life. As he would have wanted, he had a full military funeral with many of his comrades-in-arms attending, as well as hundreds of friends and citizens who had gathered at Que Que from all parts of Rhodesia. Chaplain John Fall and Reverend John Cleaver officiated and Edward Coey delivered the following eulogy on behalf of his parents standing nearby:

> When my brother left America he fully realized that the situation for us, the men of the Christian West, is as that of the Greeks at Thermopylae, as that of the Romans after Cannae, as that of Roland at Roncesvalles, as that of George Washington at Valley Forge.
>
> Yet, despite this knowledge, he came to join hands with an heroic nation, locked in mortal combat with the new barbarians. He came to strike a twofold blow: one blow against the hordes of world communism,

and one blow against the world conspiracy of money and power, which is the seducer of governments throughout the remaining free world.

He was determined that the spread of communism be stopped at the Zambezi, and he was equally determined that Western civilization never be subverted from within.

My brother came to Rhodesia on a holy mission, with a sense of destiny that his grail was here. And he has found it.

He believed that our ancient Christian code of chivalry is not dead. For it is resurrected by the greatest of Christian virtues – sacrifice.

John and scores of other Rhodesian knights have, by their sacrifice, comingled their blood with this sacred soil, and become forever saints.

But my brother did not come to Rhodesia for personal glory, and he does not desire personal glory now. For he knew that the battle was already won, and the victory already obtained 2,000 years ago on the terrible Cross of Calvary, at Golgotha, the place of the skull. He would have you know that death is glorious, yes, joyful, with faith in the Messiah, the Christ, the Son of the Living God.

To you, his comrades-in-arms, John would say, "Write these words on your hearts: The Lord is my light and my salvation, whom shall I fear? The Lord is the strength of my life, of whom shall I be afraid?

"When the wicked, even mine enemies and my foes, came upon me to eat up my flesh, they stumbled and fell. Though an host should encamp against me, my heart shall not fear. Though war should rise against me, those that seek my soul to destroy it shall go into the lower parts of the earth.

"They shall fall by the sword: they shall be a portion for foxes – and the mouth of them that speak lies shall be stopped.

"One thing have I desired of the Lord, that will I seek after, that I may dwell in the house of the Lord all the days of my life, to behold the beauty of the Lord, and to inquire in his temple.

"Wait on the Lord, be of good courage, and he shall strengthen thine heart. Wait, I say, on the Lord ..."

CHAPTER 33
Tributes

This is a representative selection of the hundreds of tributes received by John's family after the death of their son and brother.

20 July 1975

From Salisbury, Rhodesia:

> No doubt you have no idea as to who I am. I was with John in the SAS and at the School of Infantry. Having spent so much time with John I think I am qualified to say what a great chap he was.
>
> Without fear of contradiction I can say that John was a true friend to all who knew him, and a solid companion loved by all who worked with him.
>
> There is little more I can say other than the following verse fits John's deed to the fullest: 'Greater love hath no man than this that a man lay down his life for his friends'.
>
> God bless you.

From Friends in Que Que, Rhodesia:

> Our darling John has been taken away to a better land. It is very hard to take – he was so much of our own; we were his Ma and Pa here, so much like a son to us.

From Que Que, Rhodesia:

> You can be proud of John and be at peace in knowing he died the way every soldier wants to die. John knew he was going to die, because he wrote and told me. Along with that letter (in June) he sent a picture of himself out in the Valley, in uniform, machine gun under his arm. In writing about the picture, he said that that was the way he wanted me to remember him – a soldier who died for what he believed in. I think it

would be fitting and honouring in memory of John that we think of him that way.

From Columbus, Ohio, a member of John's church, St. Paul's Lutheran:

Truly. John's life, serving Christ and freedom, will be a renewed spirit for everyone who knew and loved him. John's labours, dedication and sacrifice for truth and mission work will forever be remembered. A hero beyond all heroes. A patriot beyond all patriots. Most of all a Christian, loving, doing, and living his faith.

From Redcliff, Rhodesia, a teenager:

I would like to offer my condolences to you on losing your son. I felt extremely proud, and I was moved to learn that your son had come from as far away as Ohio in the United States to help our soldiers defend Rhodesia against the evils of communism, and had lost his life in doing so. I think I can understand the grief you must be feeling because I love my country, and I'm sure your son did too, and for someone to come from America to fight for Rhodesia must surely make him the most gallant man amongst all men.

21 July 1975

From Salisbury, Rhodesia, a nurse who worked with John at the RLI hospital:

It has been a great shock and a sorrow to those of us who worked with John and knew him well. He started at the RLI soon after I did and, although it was a while before we really got to know each other, he was, one felt instinctively, the sort of person one could immediately trust and rely on. One was also impressed by the strength of character and sureness of faith in John, which led him to give up so much to come and join us here. At a time when so many lead meaningless and aimless lives, he was an outstanding contrast to others in his determination and purpose.

As a woman, I tend to decry or fight shy of those things which will involve those I love in suffering and death, and yet, I suppose if they weren't prepared to stand up for what they felt was right and true, they wouldn't be the men that we love. It's so hard to accept the loss of such a fine person, but I guess it's the way he would have had it, and I am so proud to have known him. In all the time I knew him I cannot remember ever hearing him complain. His quiet calmness and that ever-steady gaze will linger in my mind, as will his always thoughtful comments, and that ready, very hearty laugh.

As a Christian, I was delighted to learn that he too, was a Christian. It is the one thing that brings me great comfort and peace of mind – to know that he is at rest and safely in the everlasting arms of our Lord Jesus Christ. I thank and praise God that John knew and loved Him so wholeheartedly.

22 July 1975

From John's policeman friend in Bulawayo, Rhodesia:

John was a quiet, unassuming person with a strong personality which affected all who came to meet him and grew to love him. He had an impeccable character. His approach to life was always with a big grin and the extended hand of friendship with real meaning, and his love for Rhodesia and its people brought him to die for this country. He never relinquished his American citizenship, but took out his Rhodesian citizenship, of which he spoke with true pride. His presence both on our borders and at home was always a ray of sunshine.

His sturdy inner convictions of the justice of the Rhodesian war against her enemies motivated him into joining the SAS, and to enable him to play a more significant role in the aid of humanity, he became a medic. On Fireforce his presence as an active medic was a great morale booster, so inevitably, and perhaps fittingly, his death came during a recent contact in which three other members were killed, and four wounded.

John was attempting to drag to safety one wounded man when he was killed by a hail of terrorist fire. John was the hero of the action in which we have only heroes: Christianity versus communism.

From a friend in Salisbury, Rhodesia:

My deepest sympathies are with you at the loss of your son, and my friend, John.

Please do not be upset by this letter – I write simply to pay tribute to one of the finest men I have, and ever will know. There are no words which can measure up to the goodness and strength of character that were a part of John. I will never forget him.

From Salisbury, Rhodesia:

We can understand just what you are going through at the present time, as my youngest son was killed in ambush on 2 April this year, six months after his 21st birthday, and six weeks after becoming a commissioned officer.

You are probably asking yourselves the same question as I did, "Why my son?" If you are, then don't. There is no answer. Just remember and feel as proud as I am that those boys died for their ideals and their faith in their country. They gave their lives so that one day we shall have peace in Rhodesia.

Our prayers are with you. May God grant you the strength to bear this trial.

I hope you will take comfort from this verse:

'They shall grow not old, as we who are left grow old. Age shall not weary them, or the years condemn. At the going down of the sun, and in the morning. We will remember them'.

24 July 1975

From Tuscaloosa, Alabama:

We were saddened to hear of your brother's death. Although we did not know John, we feel that we were brothers in the fight to save our Christian civilization, for which he has given his life.

25 July 1975

From Colonel J.W. Drummond, Director of Medical Services, Rhodesian army:

> Words are quite inadequate at a time like this, to express my feelings as Director of Army Medical Services.
>
> Your son was a greatly valued and dedicated member of the Corps, and we are all very proud of him in that he gave his life attempting to save the lives of his fellow comrades.

27 July 1975

From Salisbury, Rhodesia, the Right Honourable Viscountess of Malvern and Bexley:

> This morning, in our church, special prayers were said for your magnificent son, John, who has given his life for my country.
>
> How proud you must be of a man, who was fighting, with his faith in God, the global evil of communism, of which my family and I are most aware and, in our small way, are also trying to combat this evil world force.

From Columbus, Ohio, where John was born and raised:

> My personal comment is that John was an extraordinary young man with great courage, noble and dedicated purpose, spiritual insight and political acumen, and keen perception of the world's affairs – far beyond his young years, and more than most men twice his age ever attain.
>
> He was truly another Christian martyr and Soldier of the Cross.

31 July 1975

From Afrikaners in Pretoria, South Africa:

> I met John recently, and what a nice young man he was. One could see from him that he was brought up as a real Christian, and that he was of very good and high character. A person one could be proud of to introduce to friends.

14 August 1975

From the secretary of Liberty Lobby Board of Policy, Washington, DC:

> How my heart bleeds for you. Although I never had the privilege of meeting John, I felt close to him. I couldn't have been prouder of him if he had been my own son. As the tears stream down my cheeks, in my heart I am rejoicing that he knew our Lord Jesus Christ as his personal Saviour. Today he is with Him.

17 August 1975

From Marandellas, Rhodesia, a Rhodesian mother:

> A chap visited us who was a radio operator in the same basecamp as your John and our son. He related an incident on one of the bush stints with John. A *picannin* (young African male child) severely injured himself whilst scaling a tree. John tended, cleaned and stitched the youngster up, all the while plying him with sweets, biscuits, etc. The chap says the medics were usually too busy to care – but not John. He was also known as 'The Fighting Doc' as he refused to stay on base.

19 August 1975

From Columbus, Ohio, a friend who had seen John grow up:

> I asked myself, why John? Then I knew the answer – John had reached spiritual perfection.
>
> I remember John at Boy Scout camp, and how much we all enjoyed seeing the programmes he was in, and seeing him in an Indian costume, dignified, proud and quiet.
>
> This poem I wrote for you, from my heart –
>
> A handsome boy in uniform
> Johnny, is that you?
> A Boy Scout teaching crafts and skills
> And love of country too.

The years passed by, as they will do,
Not many, just a few –
A man in soldier's uniform
Johnny, is that you?

Pledged to do the Lord's will
A way of life, it's true
Jesus said, 'Come home now, John'
And heaven said, 'Johnny, it is you'.

21 August 1975

From Lochem, Holland:

I had just sought to tell a Dutch girl about John's home going, when she told me there had been mention of his death in a Dutch newspaper in Amersfoort.

You are rich. Your beloved son is safe with the Lord, and when he lived on earth he was alert to what is happening. Most young men live and die with no understanding of the world, and few of them go to be with the Lord. The testimony of your family is like a bright lamp glow

ing in the darkness. God will continue to use you, I know, and John's testimony. Thank you for being my friends and thank you for standing true to God and country.

Fall of 1975

From the Honourable Lester Maddox, former governor of the State of Georgia, USA:

Although it grieves me to learn of the tragedy which took the life of your great and patriotic son, Corporal John Alan Coey, I am glad he cared so much for freedom and America. Your late son and the family he left behind are the kind of God-fearing and patriotic Americans who caused America to be great and free. He was one of those fine Americans who fought to make America a better place for me and my family, and for all

Americans to live in. I know that you must beam with love and pride, even though your loss was so great, for having had a man like him in your family, a man you could call your son. God bless you. His personal story is a great story of what he believed and fought and died for.

25 September 1975

From Salisbury, Rhodesia:

When I saw the photo in our paper of your lovely son, I wept. All my friends remarked on the beautiful sincerity and youth of his face. You can remember him always with pride as well as love.

You have left your son in a country he loved, which will always honour his memory. I am sure he would say:

And bid we both adieu and au revoir,
Since though I come no more,
I shall be waiting there to greet you
At His door.

God bless him.

He was honoured as he should be, and the cause he died for is a worthy one. These terrorists are spawns of the devil, and many thousands of Africans cannot endure the thought of the terror, chaos, and carnage if they take over.

4 July 1976

Remarks by Mr. Willis Carto at the Liberty Lobby Bicentennial Celebration Washington, DC:

This bicentennial award is presented posthumously to John Alan Coey, who has a particular place in our hearts because he gave the ultimate sacrifice. He gave of his life in the fight for freedom. He knew what he was fighting for. It is only because of the training he received at home that he did this. It is certainly our great honour to present this to his mother in his name.

3 January 1978

From Sycamore, Illinois, an American Vietnam veteran serving in the RLI, and who had lost both legs in a landmine blast:

> There are very few people in this country who can see through the smokescreen the mass media throws forth and put the real picture together. Even fewer yet will sacrifice their time and risk their lives in doing what they believe is the right thing. Without trying to inflate my own ego, I'd say John and I were two of these individuals.
>
> When I was blown up I was serving with 2 Commando, RLI, the same unit John was with when he was killed. I can't count the number of people who have asked me if I had known John Coey. Several have said we were alike in many ways. I took this as a compliment, because everyone I talked to had nothing but great respect and admiration for your son. I was very proud to fill his niche for a while.

22 March 1985

From Dr Anthony P. DiPema, author of *A Right to Be Proud*:

> I do not think John's sacrifice was in vain. There are many episodes in history where those who gave their lives in a losing cause served as an inspiration to others who eventually carried the banner to victory. The early Christian martyrs come to mind immediately. Someday, free men will learn of people like your son, John, and will realize that there were always brave men who were willing to risk their lives to keep alight the fires of freedom. Whiteaker Chambers, in his book *Witness*, makes this point in dramatic fashion.
>
> I know I will always keep John in my memories and my prayers and will relate his story of personal bravery and commitment to all who will listen, especially my own three sons.
>
> Thank you for giving me the opportunity to read John's story. His words will always remain with me. God bless you for giving the world such a wonderful son.

The funeral of Corporal John Alan Coey.

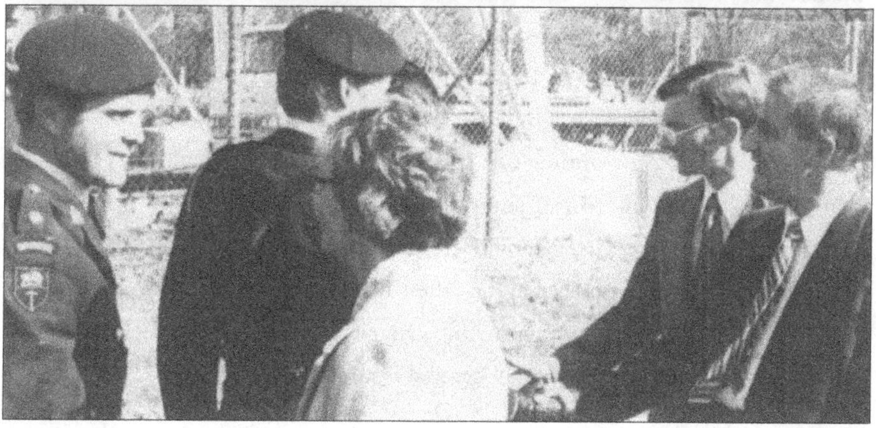

GLOSSARY OF TERMS

AD:	accidental discharge (of a weapon)
AF Hospital:	Andrew Fleming Hospital
AFA:	African Female Adult
AFJ:	African Female Juvenile
AMA:	African Male Adult
AMJ:	African Male Juvenile
APA:	African Purchase Area (Rhodesian Land Tenure Act)
APL:	African Purchase Land (Rhodesian Land Tenure Act)
AWOL:	absent without leave
BCR:	Bronze Cross of Rhodesia (equivalent to the Military Cross)
Blue Job:	airman (slang)
bombshell:	to flee or scatter in all directions (insurgent dispersal tactic on contact)
Brown Job:	soldier (slang)
BSAP:	British South Africa Police (the Rhodesian Police Force)
c/s:	call sign
cadre:	insurgent rank and file
casevac:	casualty evacuation
Charlie Tango:	Radio-speak for Communist terrorist
Chimurenga:	Shona term for the Rhodesian bush/civil war. ZANLA's 'Second War of Liberation', first used in the Mashona Rebellion of 1896, or 'The First War of Liberation'
chopper:	helicopter
CO:	Commanding Officer
COIN:	counter-insurgency
ComOps:	Combined Operations Headquarters
Cordon Sanitaire:	The minefield along the Mozambican border (Tete Province)
CQMS:	Company/Commando Quartermaster Sergeant
CSPEP:	Carrying Straps Personal Equipment Parachutist

CT: Communist terrorist
Cyclone: appointments title for Rhodesian Air Force

donga: ditch (Afrikaans)
doppie: expended cartridge case (slang)
DZ: drop zone

ek sê: I say (Afrikaans)
FAF: Forward Airfield
Fireforce: Airborne assault group
frag: fragmentation grenade
Frantan: Rhodesian euphemism for napalm
Freds: RLI slang for Frelimo (FPLM) troops
Frelimo: Mozambique Liberation Movement (*Frente de Libertaçâo de Moçambique*)

G-car: troop-ferrying helicopter, normally an Alouette III, armed with twin .303 Brownings or 7.62 MAGs
gomo: hill or *kopje* (Shona)
gook: insurgent (American military slang from Korea)
graze: to eat or food (RLI slang)

HE: high-explosive
HMG: heavy machine gun
hondo: war, conflict (Shona)

Intaf: Ministry of Internal Affairs (abbreviation)
IO: Intelligence Officer

jesse: thick thorn scrub
JOC: Joint Operations Centre

K-car: 'Killer car', helicopter command gunship, normally an Alouette III, equipped with 20mm cannon

KIA: killed in action
kopje: hill (Afrikaans—pronounced 'copy', also *koppie*)
kraal: African village (South African corruption of the Portuguese *curral* meaning a cattle pen or enclosure)

lemon: term for an aborted or botched-up call-out/operation. (Rhodesian Security Force slang)
loc: location or position
locstat: positional co-ordinates
LZ: landing zone.

MAG: *matireurs à gas*—gas-operated, belt-fed section machine gun, manufactured by Fabrique Nationale (FN, Belgium) and used by Rhodesian Security Forces
MFC: Military Forces Commendation
mielies: maize cobs (Afrikaans, also mealies)
MO: Medical Officer
MT: Motor Transport
MTO: Motor Transport Officer
mujiba: young insurgent supporter, the insurgents' 'eyes and ears' (Shona)
NCO: Non-Commissioned Officer
NS: National Serviceman
OC: Officer Commanding
OP: observation post
ops: operations

PATU: Police Anti-Terrorist Unit (BSAP para-military COIN specialist unit)
PF: Patriotic Front (ZANU/ZAPU alliance)
PJI: Parachute Jump Instructor
povo: people (Portuguese, and now commonly Shona)
PRAW: Police Reserve Air Wing
PRI: President Regimental Institute/Institution

PTS:	Parachute Training School
PV:	Protected Village
R&R:	Rest & Recreation (also as Rest & Retraining/Relaxation/ Recuperation/Refitting etc.)
R/L:	Ringer's lactate
RAR:	Rhodesian African Rifles
RBC:	Rhodesian Broadcasting Corporation
RF:	Rhodesian Front, white political party headed by Ian Smith
RhAF:	Rhodesian Air Force
RLI:	Rhodesian Light Infantry
RR:	Rhodesia Regiment (white territorial battalions numbered 1 to 10)
RSM:	Regimental Sergeant-Major
SAP:	South African Police
SAS:	Special Air Service
SB:	Special Branch (of the BSAP)
SCR:	Silver Cross of Rhodesia
SF:	Rhodesian Security Forces
sitrep:	situation report
Sneb:	air-to-ground attack rocket
stick:	four-man battle group, an Alouette helicopter troop-load, originally five men but the fifth man made way for helicopter machine guns. Originally from a stick of paratroopers
'take the gap':	Rhodesian Security Force expression used to denote a rapid exit from a location
terr:	terrorist
TF:	Territorial Force
TTL:	Tribal Trust Land/s (Rhodesian Land Tenure Act)
UANC:	United African National Council, headed by Bishop Abel Muzorewa
UDI:	Unilateral Declaration of Independence

vlei:	swampy, open grassland (Afrikaans)
WO:	Warrant Officer
WP:	white phosphorus
ZANLA:	Zimbabwe African National Liberation Army, ZANU's military wing
ZANU:	Zimbabwe African National Union, headed by Robert Mugabe
ZAPU:	Zimbabwe African People's Union, headed by Joshua Nkomo
ZIPRA:	Zimbabwe People's Revolutionary Army, ZAPU's military wing
ZNA:	Zimbabwe National Army